*Just
take it
from
the Lord,
brother*

Just take it from the Lord, brother

Jeanette Lockerbie

Fleming H. Revell Company
Old Tappan, New Jersey

Library of Congress Cataloging in Publication Data

Lockerbie, Jeanette W
Just take it from the Lord, brother.

1. Providence and government of God. 2. Christian life—1960– I. Title.
BT135.L6   231'.5   74-18021
ISBN 0-8007-0698-6

TO
my friends whose shared
experiences have given me
much insight into how we
"take things from the Lord."

.

Contents

Introduction

One of the glories of being a human is that we have the power of choice. We can choose to take things—from God and from each other. Or, we can go through life asserting our independence, or suspecting everybody—and the Lord—of having ulterior motives in making things available to us.

"What does 'Just take it from the Lord' mean to you," I asked a number of people, in the course of writing this book.

"It's an expression of superpiety," said one person.

"Saying 'Just take it from the Lord' is a cop-out," another told me. "It's what we say when we don't want to get involved with someone else's problems."

"It may be all right for you. But for me? Forget it," was how a young fellow answered.

It was sad to realize that quite a few I talked with equated taking something from God with taking some evil-tasting medicine.

There were others, though, who had a more positive attitude.

"What does it mean?" a bright-eyed teen-ager responded. "It means that since God is my heavenly Father, He loves me. It's no problem for me just to take things from Him."

One woman told me as she observed how her husband accepted God's will for him—how God could apparently *trust* her husband with sickness—that she herself learned to take things from the Lord.

A few I queried had Job's philosophy: I have received good at the hand of God; shall I not also accept evil? But for the most part, the response was negative. It certainly puts the Almighty in a bad light. Some betrayed their own low self-concept by their attitude, "Why should God send anything good *my* way? Who am I?"

Why is this? I wondered. What in the person's makeup and background has conditioned and programmed him for purely negative responses?

Why should something that comes from the heart and hand of God not be good for us? To be sure, the phrase "Act of God" has done nothing to make God look like the Benefactor of mankind that He is. Yet it takes but a few seconds to recount in our minds a host of acts of God that bless us both day and night. The fact that the sun comes up in the morning, the rain refreshes, a rose sweetens our day, a landscape causes us to hold our breath in delight, a star-filled night fills us with wonder; these and a myriad more acts of God add beauty and zest to our lives—to say nothing of the material gifts of God that sustain us throughout our days.

How, then, can we so quickly view what God sends us as suspect? As though our Father is more interested in making stoics of His people than of lovingly providing for our needs and more.

Do we, by our quiet acceptance or petulant questioning, influence our brother's or sister's ability to take things from the Lord? It would appear that we do.

Generally we don't have to be convinced that what comes from the devil is evil. Why not the reverse: "If it comes from God, it surely must be good"?

In this day of current shortages are we perhaps guilty, consciously or unconsciously, of thinking that God, too, is affected in His ability to supply good things for His children; that He "can't afford it"?

What, among our basic concepts, governs our ability to "take it from the Lord"?

It's profitable, spiritually and emotionally, for us to take out our too-trite sayings—spread them out on the table of our mind—mentally finger them and evaluate them and what they are doing to us in a practical way.

In these chapters we have attempted to work through some of the broad ramifications and deep implications of the seemingly glib and simple suggestion, "Just take it from the Lord, brother."

JEANETTE LOCKERBIE

Just take it from the Lord, brother

1

You Can Take It—It's From Me

There's something glib and casual in the way one Christian will say to another, "Just take it from the Lord, brother."

Frequently there can be detected a hint of "I'm glad it's you and not me!" It is as though, although we wouldn't put it in these words, we may be saying, "If it's from the Lord, it just might not be something I would appreciate, so—I pass."

One of the problems of being able to take something from the Lord is, *How do I know it is from the Lord?* It's important to know this. How often, for example, when someone's words or actions might otherwise rattle us, we shrug them off with, "Consider the source"?

Not only God but Satan also has a big stake in what we do, how we act as professed Christians. And Satan has his fiery darts all at the ready to aim at us. We need to be discerning, then, as to where things come from that affect us.

I was interested a few days ago as I listened and participated in a discussion over a cup of coffee. Much was being said about, "Satan's at the root of the whole thing"; "The devil has it in for us Christians," —and more of the same. This is true. But there's another side to it. One young fellow chipped in with, "I'm not gonna give Satan all the credit."

We need some means of gauging where things come from.

The Bible gives at least one instance where a troublesome thing is part of the story. And the Lord takes direct responsibility for the source.

The Lord had revealed Himself to Moses by the burning bush in the desert. God then acknowledged that He had heard the cry of Moses' people for deliverance, and right there He tapped Moses on the shoulder for the job of emancipator. Very obviously, Moses would like to have said, "I pass, Lord." He put forth a number of excuses: "Who am I?" among them. Moses felt he was just not the man for the position. Even when God performed the two-way miracle of changing a rod into a serpent, then reversing the procedure, Moses didn't get excited at being chosen. His final excuse was his lack of eloquence (*see* Exodus 4:10). (Some Bible scholars agree that actually Moses suffered from a speech defect: Legend has it that the child Moses in Pharaoh's palace burned his tongue severely enough to cause this to affect his speech for the rest of his life.)

Whatever the cause or the extent of Moses' limitations as a speaker, it was enough, in his own thinking, to disqualify him. But God was not to be put off. In effect, God said that whatever Moses was, He, the Lord, had made him (*see* 4:11) and having thus taken all the responsibility, God moved to provide Moses with a spokesman (rather than, as Moses would have preferred, an *out*).

It was a long, hard haul, but God was there with Moses in every trial along the way. There was a time when Moses would have appreciated knowing a little more about what was ahead of him, and who wouldn't be right there asking God for the same preview of our tomorrows! God knows us better than we know ourselves, however. When Moses asked, "Show me thy way and show me thy glory" (*see* Exodus 33:13, 18), the Lord knew better than to do either one. If He had shown Moses the way He had mapped out for him, Moses would likely have fainted at the prospect of drought and heat and long years of desert travel with a rebellious, fretful host of people to command. And if God had shown Moses His glory, Moses might well have been useless for earth, so eager would he have been to enjoy the glories of heaven. God did answer. God always answers. In Moses' case He answered the request with an unconditional promise, "My presence shall go with thee, and I will give thee rest" (v.14).

Moses would always know that whatever came his way he could

take from the Lord for he had God's personal promise of reinforcement for his journey.

How can *we* be sure of where our trials come from?

One way we can know is that when God sends a trial, He goes through it with us, as He did with Moses and others of the patriarchs and some ordinary people in Bible times. By contrast, when Satan is the instigator, he adds his innuendoes against God; he prods the person he has selected for his victim and urges him to rebel against God and blame God for his problems. Sometimes Satan will even use those closest to us to try to accomplish his diabolical schemes. You will recall that it was Job's *wife* who said to her husband in the midst of his sorrow and anguish, ". . .curse God and die" (Job 2:9). The time came when he did curse the day he was born (*see* 3:1–4), but Job knew better than to take such counsel as his wife offered, that he curse God. Even in his afflicted state, Job's mind saw the logic of being able to take good things from the Lord as being a reasonable explanation of why we should take evil, likewise, from the Lord if it is His will to send it. Curse God? Never!

A family of my acquaintance has a mentally retarded child. Born apparently healthy in every respect, he developed normally until the age of two. Then severe symptoms began to appear. Soon the lovely little boy lost his power of speech and failed to develop in other areas. He became increasingly incapacitated until it became evident that it would be best for him and for his heartbroken parents that he be cared for in an institution.

The day came when the long car with the attendant from the hospital arrived. ("It's best if you do not bring him," the kindly social worker had suggested. "You just might decide not to leave him.") As the car rounded the corner out of sight, the grieving parents sought relief in their Bible.

"I'm no theologian," said the father, in relating the sad events of that day to me. "I cannot fathom the ways of God. I read Psalms 77:2: 'In the day of my trouble I sought the Lord,' and as I read on, the Word of God comforted us. I don't know how. I just know it did. When I came to the verse that reads, 'Hath God forgotten to be

gracious?' (v. 9), I could read on, 'I will remember the works of the
Lord' (v.11). He had been gracious. He had not forgotten us. To my
mind came a hymn I had learned as a boy, 'Blessed be the Name,
Blessed be the Name of the Lord.' I knew it came from a Bible verse,
so I looked it up and found that Job had said it: 'The Lord gave, and
the Lord hath taken away; blessed be the name of the Lord' " (Job
1:21).

It was at nightfall that the sense of loss almost swamped this father.
When he came upon his little son's stuffed puppy that he always took
to bed, he just sat down and wept. "And in that moment," he states,
"as clearly as if God had knocked on the door and announced His
presence, He spoke to me. I heard His voice saying, 'Ben, be of good
cheer.' The Lord stood by me that night as surely as He stood by Paul
on the storm-tossed ship's deck."

That family has weathered the storm of having their beloved child
isolated from them; never hearing his voice; visiting him and yet not
having a son in the sense that a family enjoys a child's presence. They
took this living sorrow as from the Lord; they looked to Him for
strength and endurance and comfort—and they found it. Like many
another, they have proven the truth of the beautiful, haunting new
hymn,

> Through it all, through it all
> I've learned to trust in Jesus,
> I have learned to trust in God . . .

and as they have trusted the Lord in the midst of strong trial, they've
been a blessing and a source of sustenance to other parents in like
circumstances.

Perhaps God's voice can best be heard in the furnace of affliction.
For, as C.S. Lewis so aptly phrased it, "[Pain] is [God's] megaphone
to rouse a deaf world."

No matter how much we learn, how much we are refined through
sorrow, it still is not fair to God to portray Him as sending only
shadows into our lives. God is the God of sunshine just as much as
He is the God of rain. The Bible tells us He has given us richly all

things to enjoy. God is interested in our enjoyment.

Have you watched a child as someone has offered him a lavish gift? The child looks to his mother with a should-I-take-it ambivalence: wanting to grasp the gift in his hands, but sensing that it's too much. Some of us have this attitude toward God, as though He just dispenses pennies, or nickel candy. We have a wary attitude about taking some of His greater gifts.

"Taking it from the Lord" is a many-faceted matter and for every person who has a reasonable attitude toward such things there is almost surely someone whose ideas are distorted.

For some strange reason it's difficult for some people to accept good things as coming from God. It may be that some of us have been conditioned (by parents or through the teachings of our church) to expect deprivations as Christians: It's almost as though "doing without" is a prerequisite to security in the afterlife; as though one were paying for the other.

Nothing can be further from the truth. The Bible abounds in examples of men rich in this world's goods, yet who were important in God's program and who enjoyed His blessings. Abraham is a prime example, with flocks and herds and servants; David, "a man after God's own heart," was a *king,* and Job, when we first encounter him and again as we take leave of him in the Bible, was an influential and wealthy landowner. (Even Satan said to God, "Look how rich he is" [*see* Job 1:10].)

In the early days of the church and ever since, God has had men and women whom He could trust not to be snared away from their love for Him through prosperity and wealth.

Why should it be unusual for God's people to enjoy His bounty in a material way? Does not our God own the cattle on a thousand hills? It's not money itself, but the *love of money* that is "the root of all evil" according to the Scriptures (1 Timothy 6:10). ". . . if riches increase, set not your heart upon them" (Psalms 62:10).

Material possessions need have little to do with one's relationship to God and to Jesus Christ.

Sometimes we hear questions like, "Where did *you* get a thing like that? Did you rob a bank?" The setting usually is that of a Christian showing something he's just bought or otherwise acquired. The reaction of his friends when he shows the object says, in essence, "That's more than a Christian should have," or, "The Lord had nothing to do with your acquiring that thing." Disapproval sounds out in both statements.

An awful thought strikes me. Can it be that we don't really *believe* that God loves us? In our human circles the greatest evidence that we are loved is that someone lavishes the best he has upon us. Feeling loved by God, we should be able to take *all He has to offer us.*

Or, do we believe we are not really worthy of God's love, so we cannot accept His gifts of good things along the way through life?

Surely the Lord would want us to be balanced Christians, able to take the good and to take adversity, not letting either one dim our view of God.

There are some who are scripturally off-center. They can take only the good from the Lord. They are the people who say, "I can't believe a God of love would let His children suffer. I can't buy that" (nor will they take it for nothing).

Well, *Jesus* believed a God of love would let His Son suffer.

> . . . the cup which my Father hath given me, shall I not drink it?
>
> John 18:11

Jesus knew full well where the sorrow came from and *He* took it from God.

In "drinking the cup," Jesus purchased for us the world's all-time greatest gift, the gift of salvation and eternal life with Him in heaven.

"You can take it; it's from me," Jesus is saying to us today. Of salvation we can confidently say to another person,

"Just take it from the Lord, brother!"

2

What Else Can I Expect?

We tend to program ourselves according to what we expect from life. And all too often this determines our ability to take what God sends to us day-by-day.

I have a friend, a busy executive, who is a habitual early riser. When people comment on this custom, his eyes twinkle as he explains, "I *have* to get up early in the morning. I can hardly wait to see what God is up to!" His attitude of expectancy makes him look for good things. He is one of those who regard every tomorrow as the great possibility.

There are others, however, who are pure pessimists. For whatever reason, theirs is a gloomy outlook toward life. They perennially expect the worst. It may be that, as children, their good expectations were crushed. They've grown up without ever once having owned a pair of rose-colored glasses. In the growing-up process they've become cynical, never expecting anything but the negative. After a while, when this is realized repeatedly, the person internalizes and personalizes the experiences and begins to think in terms of "What else can I expect?" (The connotation always to his disadvantage, in his own mind.)

Unless we can separate the experience from ourselves as persons, the danger is that we will see every disappointment in life as, "What else can I expect?" The vicious cycle then is strengthened as the person's cynical expectations become self-fulfilling. He sees himself as not being worthy of having nice, good, pleasant things happen to him. This, in turn, causes other people to regard him as they see him regard himself.

We don't learn this lesson in school. Some people never learn it. I admit to having learned it from my own son. (If you have read my book, *The Image of Joy,* you may recall the incident.) My self-esteem was at a low ebb and I was apprehensive about entering into a totally new experience. And my son, Bruce, said to me, gently, "Remember, Mother, these people are strangers; they will view you and accept you exactly as they see you accepting yourself." I found this to be both profound and true. My son's love-motivated statement caused me to do some self-evaluating. The outcome was that I saw myself as a most favored person, a child of the King, the beneficiary of countless promises if I would only appropriate them. God loved me and cared what happened to me. My times were in His hands.

Such pondering can't help but build one's self-image!

When we see a person who is confident, poised, seemingly able to roll with the punches, ride the waves of what life brings, we have good feelings toward this person. We trust him because he appears to be able to believe in himself.

Conversely, one who appears not to believe in himself, and who carries this into his everyday behavior and his contacts with other people, generally has problems with others. They see him as only negative, and since most people have enough negatives in their lives, they don't want to have other people's unhealthy attitudes constantly rub off on them. The pessimist rarely has friends. Oh, he may have people who feel sorry for him, but not people who seek him out to make a friend of him. He may even have some genuinely fine qualities but he is projecting all the wrong ones. He doesn't trust the abilities God has given him; he doesn't trust what other people do; he is always on the lookout for someone to cheat him or otherwise do him wrong. This is one of his chronic expectations.

Another characteristic of this person is that he can never accept genuine praise. Why? Because there's never enough of it. He turns it down. But his "Who, me! You can't mean *me,*" is all too often a bid for more and greater praise. When this is not forthcoming (for people get tired of such tactics), he shrugs and sighs, "What else can I expect?"

He expects life to hand him a raw deal and not surprisingly, this often happens. The Christian is no exception and his poor expectations extend, illogically, even as to how *God* will treat him. And yet, as Christians we have reason for having the greatest of all expectations. David said, "My soul, wait thou only upon God; for my expectation is from him" (Psalms 62:5). The psalmist knew where to look. His expectations had the right source for fulfillment.

Such great expectations keep us in a spirit of happy excitement. (I have heard it said that when Mark Twain was asked the secret of his success in life, he answered, "I was born *excited.*")

Each day can bring its own excitement. The Christian life is the most exciting life of all. When we commit our lives totally to the Lord, it's not some kind of cold resignation to the inevitable, as some believers might cause the non-Christian to suppose. Oh, no! No robots are we. God has given us a mind and a will and He expects that we will exercise both. Committing our life to Him puts us into direct partnership with the Creator, the Author of creativity. And He has a creative program for every one of us who wants to get in on it. This should keep us on tiptoe, eager to do His will.

Sometimes *I* can hardly wait to see what God is going to do in my life next! I recall, a couple of years ago, when the book *Daktar* was just beginning to be thought about by publishers, each day for a month an exciting piece of God's plan came to view. It started (as far as my going to the brand-new nation of Bangladesh was concerned) with a nagging feeling that I must apply for a passport. A Scottish-born Canadian citizen living in the United States can have delay problems with Immigration, and my passport had expired. But I wasn't going anywhere! Nevertheless I couldn't get away from the urge to do something about it. At the time, I mentioned this to a friend and she said, "Where are you going that you need a passport?" "Nowhere, I just feel I should go ahead and apply for one," was my answer. (Later, she reminded me that I'd said this.) The book about the Olsens had been started in my mind years before; I had a store of material in my files concerning the brilliant doctor and his unusually gifted wife. A number of obstacles had to be overcome, but in exciting ways God worked them out. Almost daily, my friends and colleagues at the Narramore Foundation would ask expectantly, "What's God doing for you today, Jeanette?" And I never had to search my mind for a ready answer. So numerous were the unexplainable "coincidences" that I listed them in writing so I would never forget.

God's plan for us does not often take us halfway around the world. But at home, He can meet our expectations with just as much excitement. Our family, for instance, every one of us, has an undying excitement about the *mail.* We laugh about it and tease each other, asking, What *are* you expecting? when one of us drops everything to see what the mailman's brought. I'm sure it's not an exclusively Lockerbie trait. And for those who possess it, it leads to great expectations. I know other people, though, who have only negative expectations: Even while the mailman is still half a block away they're saying to themselves, "He won't be bringing *me* anything." Then, when he does leave mail, before they even look at it, they speculate, "Oh, it won't be anything worthwhile—junk mail, likely, or somebody asking for something." A totally negative outlook. Our family, on the other hand, probably because we have had many happy things in the mail, can shrug off one bad day, thinking, *Well, not much today*—(never "What else can I expect?"). *But there's tomorrow.* And up goes our expectation barometer.

This is such a good, emotionally healthy way to live. For—think of it!—the very next minute, hour, and day has a *50 percent* chance of being *good;* being exciting; happy. It could be bad—but the chances are even that it will be good. For the Christian this is the only way to think. Everything God has ever promised is for our positive, ultimate good. "I know the thoughts that I think toward you, saith the Lord, thoughts of peace, and not of evil, to give you an expected end" (Jeremiah 29:11).

Great expectations! And what of ". . . all things work together for good . . ." (Romans 8:28)? Not that each individual experience, each incident in our life is good (as is pointed out in the chapter on "Acceptance"). The warp and woof of our life calls for both bright strands and drab, as is so well expressed in these lines from the poem, *The Weaver.*

> Not till the loom is silent
> And the shuttle has ceased to fly,
> And God has unrolled the canvas and explained
>   the reason why

The dark threads are as needful
In the Weaver's skillful hands,
As the threads of gold and silver
In the pattern He has planned.

We never know at what moment God is going to drop a thread of gold into the seeming drabness of a life. We do know that it does take both kinds, the bright and the dark, even as it takes both sunshine and rain to balance nature.

There will come days when it may seem that the clouds will never lift; the sun brighten our lives no more. Such are the "things" that we're called on to endure. But God will take the "things." I know, for I've proven Him many times. I've learned to trust Him. So I expect God to work in the circumstance until the total experience does become good. And—do you know what? This just gives me all the more faith to expect for the next time!

The Scripture says, "According to your faith be it unto you" (Matthew 9:29), so there is a distinct correlation between faith and expectancy.

Perhaps we would do well to examine our expectations. I have a friend, a mature, devout Christian—she has been president of the Women's Auxiliary of the Gideons International—and every time we meet I can be certain she will ask, with a happy smile, "Had any spiritual surprises lately?" Sometimes she calls them "serendipities."

I can honestly say, "Yes, Edie, as a matter of fact I have," and I stop to tell her about them—the good things God sends my way.

How much success you or I will have is undoubtedly tied into our expectations of what God is going to do *for* us, and *in* us and *through* us. Perhaps one of the best ways we can demonstrate the reality of our Christian faith is to be full of expectancy, using each hour as a kind of springboard for enjoying what God has to offer.

It's a great life being a Christian! Because it's so true that we get out of life just what we expect, why not go all out for great expectations? Everything we know about God tells He will honor our good expectations. We're not dealing with blind optimism, nor with variables of possibilities. We're dealing in the realm of known factors: God's love, His caring for us, His interest in us, and the fact that He knows our "expected end."

Paul the Apostle speaks of his "earnest expectation and . . . hope" (Philippians 1:20). He ties these together. You and I can, too. Like Paul, we can live with high hopes.

Parents, if they are on the alert for signs of positive and negative attitudes on the part of their children, can help while the child is still young to steer him in the direction of good expectations. He is then likely to grow up with happy excitement about tomorrow, capable of feeling worthy of having nice things happen to him.

A word of caution: Parents need to be careful that children have realistic expectations, that they are not living in a fairy-tale world where everyone lives happily ever after. They need to know that life is not like that. When we are not realistic—and, to a degree, when we are—we're bound to experience disappointments from time to time. But this need not make us feel, "What else could I expect?"

There's nothing misplaced about our expectations as to what God can and will do for us. When we're tuned into Him, we'll never have cause to downgrade ourselves, to feel unworthy of having good things happen to us as if we couldn't expect anything else but the worst.

Living for and with God is the greatest of all adventures.

3

Better Than the Dow Jones Averages

For some people who are introduced to Christianity as an adult, it is also an introduction to a new vocabulary. I distinctly recall being initiated into a new set of words all of which began with *omni*: omni*potent*—omni*presence*—omni*science,* among others. It doesn't take much familiarity with Latin to get the sense of the prefix. But it sometimes takes long years before the Christian personalizes and internalizes their meaning.

The very majesty of the words, which can apply only to God, sets God apart as "Other" and tends to keep us from analyzing these *omnis* for ourselves. It took lean times as a minister's wife for me to learn, for instance, that God is *omnipotent.* I'm afraid that, like many another, my estimate of God's ability to provide for His own was poles apart from what the Bible so clearly states: ". . . according to his riches" (Philippians 4:19)—not our lack of them!

Because we are limited to our human perspective, we may be tempted to think (though we would not put it in these words) that God "cannot afford it." Ours is a generation of rising prices and shortages to the extent that this has become a thought pattern to many of us. We need a fresh realization that our God is not limited by any of these things that restrict man. And we've taken a giant step of faith when we recognize with our heart as well as with our mind that *God can* afford it. Some of us, perhaps, need the lesson poetically taught by the astute sparrow, in dialogue with a robin. Having considered the grubbing and fretting of the human species over fear of material lack,

Said the Robin to the Sparrow:
    "I should really like to know
Why these anxious human beings
Rush about and worry so."

Said the Sparrow to the Robin:
    "Friend, I think that it must be
That they have no heavenly Father
Such as cares for you and me."
                              ELIZABETH CHENEY

All too often, by our overconcern we do give this impression to other people and we allow it to cloud our own thinking. Our lack of comprehension of the riches in Jesus needn't make us doubt that there's enough and more. God's supply is in no way affected by current shortages, interest rates, or the Dow Jones averages: it has nothing to do with the things that invade our minds when we dwell on the problems of supply and demand and overpopulation and its attendant fears.

We can't know the size or square footage of God's storehouse. We cannot count the riches of Jesus. We *can* count on God's promise. His Word tells us, "But my God shall supply all your need . . ." (Philippians 4:19). That *but* is one of the good *buts* of the Bible. It's saying to us, in essence, "Other sources may fail you; other wells dry up; but —my God (the God whom the Apostle Paul had proven to be sufficient for his every need) shall supply *your* need." I've heard it quipped, "God has promised to supply all our need—not our greed." But that's another matter (though worth thinking about here and now).

It's of extreme importance that we never lose sight of how God is keeping that promise to supply our every need. Remembering always that it is through His riches in Jesus will keep us from the frenzy of fears as costs escalate and there seems no end in sight.

It's not according to the Dow Jones, but according to God's supply.

Sometimes, all unwittingly, we give wrong impressions to people around us. I'm reminded of a situation where I sat at breakfast with a lovely Christian family. Their young granddaughter was visiting. Knowing her grandparents' custom of reading the Bible with the family around the breakfast table, she asked, "Grandpa, can *I* get the Bible today?" She was excused and she slipped off her chair and ran into the living room to get the Bible. As she laid it at her grandfather's place, he rose from the table and went toward the radio. Then, turning to the little girl, he said, "We'll read the Bible in a few minutes, honey. But Grandpa doesn't want to miss the stock market report. It's just coming on."

This grandfather would not, for worlds, have willingly put any kind of a stumbling block in front of his granddaughter. He and his wife made every effort to see that she was spiritually nurtured. It just did not occur to him that later on—if not now—this girl might view family devotions as second in importance to the Dow Jones averages. For, moments later, she heard her grandfather express his prayer that God would provide the needs of each one around that table; give them their daily bread. But first he had sought for assurance through the stock market.

Sometimes even when we're praying for a certain thing, we have in mind where God can procure it for us and if we were totally honest in our prayer it might go something like this: "Lord, You know I want (whatever it is), and, God, it's at . . ."and we would describe the place and give God the details such as how much it costs.

Very often the things that God most wants to give us "richly to enjoy" are commodities that will never be listed on the world's stock market, for they are the intangibles: peace, joy, contentment—these money cannot buy. And no man has a corner on them.

Jesus ennunciated a great principle with His, "But seek ye first the kingdom of God, and his righteousness; and all these things shall be added unto you" (Matthew 6:33).

One Sunday after the Sunday-school session, I asked a few of the adult class members it was my privilege to teach, to be ready to share with us the following week the best piece of advice they had ever received. The response was good. Each one whom I had asked gave a specific instance. One I have never forgotten. A very young married woman, Lois, told of how, in the years when her husband was still a college student, their finances were so low that she was in a constant state of apprehension. What if she got sick? What if, after all the grind of college, her husband didn't get the engineering position for which he was training? These and other "what ifs" plagued her, giving her no peace. Then, she related to us, a neighbor who was likewise a Christian, sensing Lois's dilemma, told her that she, herself, had been on the same treadmill of fear and worry.

Asked how she overcame the problem, this neighbor had replied, "It may seem overly simple to you, but it has worked and is working for me."

Lois explained that her neighbor had reached for a Bible lying on the coffee table and, opening it to Matthew chapter 6, said, "Read that verse." Lois complied and read the familiar "But seek ye first the kingdom of God, and his righteousness; and all these things shall be added unto you" (v. 33).

The neighbor related that one day, loaded with fears for the day and apprehension for the future, she had come across this verse. "I decided to take God at His Word," she explained. "I didn't know what in a practical sense it meant to seek first God's kingdom and His righteousness. But whatever it was, I told God, I was willing to do it if He would only help me. That day a great new peace came over me, body, soul, and spirit. I can't explain it. Every day from that day till this, when I wake up in the morning I just thank God that He is in control of my life and ask Him to help me keep my mind on Him, to seek first the kingdom. It works. It's working for me—and you should try it."

"And that," Lois summed up, "is the best piece of advice I ever received. It revolutionized my life. It's been just wonderful!" For the never-an-idle-moment mother of little children this might sometimes have to be this prayer that I read recently on a wall hanging,

Lord, You know how busy I will be today.
If I forget You, please do not forget me.

Like the helpful and honest neighbor, probably most of us have given but cursory attention to Matthew 6:33, in part because of our familiarity with it as a Sermon-on-the-Mount verse. But after hearing this piece of advice, I began to seriously meditate on "But seek ye first the kingdom of God. . . ." Somehow the word *first* assumed new proportions. What exactly did Jesus mean by it? I realize it's presumptuous to suppose that you or I can read the mind of Christ (and yet are we not exhorted to have the mind of Christ? *See* Philippians 2:5).

Did Jesus mean first in respect to *time?* Was He speaking of first thing in the morning?

Did He mean first in the sense of our priorities: first on our TO DO TODAY list—every day?

Or—and this was a brand-new insight, for me—was our Lord inferring that there is a kind of stewardship other than that of our time and our talents and our worldly goods? I found myself dwelling on the possibility that Jesus was teaching a stewardship of our *mental processes.* Obviously this is the core of our problems of anxiety about today and tomorrow: about the clothes and the food Jesus had mentioned (Matthew 6:31, 32).

In bidding us seek first the kingdom of God, it seems to me Jesus was saying, in essence, that before the cares and the worries and the burdens of the day would bow us down, we should consciously and deliberately put our mind to the task of concentrating on God. A kingdom presupposes a king. He is our King; we are His subjects. He is, therefore, ultimately responsible for our welfare. As we feed this kind of thinking into our psyche, it will prevent preoccupation with the cares of the day from taking root in our heart and mind, controlling us much of the day.

This line of thought is corroborated by Isaiah the prophet when he said, "Thou wilt keep him in perfect peace, whose mind is stayed on thee: because he trusteth in thee" (26:3). Ah, there is the crux of the matter. Because he *trusts.*

Why should we trust? Why, indeed! Because our God is not only a King ruling His kingdom; He is a Father caring for His children. Jesus said so. ". . . your heavenly Father knoweth that ye have need of all these things [food, drink, clothes]" (Matthew 6:32).

And knowing, He cares.

All of this and more was inherent in Lois's "best piece of advice."
It worked for her as it did for her neighbor. It has worked for me,
I assure you.

Are you responding in your mind with, *It's all right for you, and
for other women. But I'm a busy executive. I have lots to worry about:
the tightness of money, increasing shortages of materials to work with,
indifferent employees—and, oh, a hundred other things that harass me.*

I'm so glad that Christ's promise covers your case, too, for you do
have great needs. It seems the more successful a person becomes, the
greater are his frustrations in the business world. I might not have
been able to speak to your reasonable objection to this simple formula
for peace of mind. This very morning, however, I listened as the head
of a large financial corporation addressed a group of executives. At
one point he said that he is frequently asked for his definition of
success and that on one occasion he found himself saying, "Success
is being in the will of God." He had not pondered the question before
answering as he would normally do. The words had just come out,
surprising himself. "But," he said to this group of fellow high-pow-
ered businessmen, "I've never come up with a more satisfactory definition of success."

What better way, we might ponder, to be in the will of God than
by daily seeking first the kingdom of God and His righteousness?

In these days, just thinking about the righteousness of God, that He
is just, that He will treat us justly, should be a tremendous source of
inner security. For all too many people today are feeling—some saying, "There's no justice anymore."

I think that most of us can tolerate many other things more than
we can tolerate injustice when it affects us personally or affects those
whom we love.

God is a righteous God and He treats us with righteousness. Since
we are what we think (*see* Proverbs 23:7), thinking and meditating on
these great, expansive areas of God's kingdom and righteousness will
preclude morbid dwelling on negatives that would rob us of peace.
The resultant freedom from worry, fretting, and apprehension as to
the future will give us a new contentment, peace, and joy. And this

cannot but increase one's effectiveness—in business and in interpersonal relations, and in personal well-being. Such increased effectiveness will ultimately lead to a greater measure of success.

Some doubts and fears may still, from time to time, ruffle us on the surface. We might as well be realistic about that. But we need never let them invade our minds, take root and swamp us, controlling our day.

Are you looking for some sound advice? Try this Matthew 6:33 formula. The omnipotent, the all-powerful, all-seeing, ever present heavenly Father is our surety for the success of this formula. He knows our needs. He cares. And He can well afford to supply our needs.

It beats depending on the Dow Jones averages.

4

The God of the Special Touch

Some people need more assurance than others. This can be seen in children in the same family. A father I know told me, "I can just pat my older little boy on the head as I walk past him. But that won't do for his brother. I have to pick him up and pet him a bit." And there is a wise father, to recognize the different needs of his own children.

Our heavenly Father knows what we need, and He, too, is there with His special touch. But some Christians go through life without ever knowing this; they think God has one prescribed treatment for all of us. Or, which is probably worse, they feel unworthy of special attention from God. Usually this stems from their early impressions of God, picked up from others around them. Take Stan, for example. As a college freshman he heard the gospel and believed. His profession of Christ was sincere and honest. But a month or so later he walked over to where his friend (who had influenced him to listen to the gospel message) was seated on the grassy campus. "Here. You gave this to me. You can have it back," he said with a mixture of defiance and wistfulness, and he tossed a New Testament down alongside his friend.

"What d'you mean—you're giving up?" Tom asked.

"Just that. The standard's too high for me, Tom. Can't live up to it."

He would have stalked off. But Tom jumped to his feet and stepped in front of Stan, blocking his path momentarily. "C'mon, man! Let's talk about it."

Tom didn't argue. He listened, and after a while the picture was clear to him. Stan was a fellow whose image of God was that of a strong, rigidly disciplining Creator who stands over His creatures, if not with a stick to keep them in line, then certainly with a tape recorder to keep track of every infraction, every omission, every transgression—and remembers them forever more. (It would take a Christian psychiatrist or psychologist just one brief session to trace where *this* kind of thinking sprang from. We see God as we view our own father, these professionals tell us. How important, then, that a Christian father projects the right image of God to his children.)

With the image Stan had of God, it was natural that his thinking concerning God's dealings with him would be warped. And since even after his conversion, Stan realized he was tempted and that he could still be guilty of doing some of the things that had troubled his conscience in his preconversion days, he figured that God would give up on him. Stan's giving up was, in a sense, to beat God giving *him* up. He didn't know the kind of God he had placed his faith in. Not knowing the Bible, he was not aware that "The Lord is merciful and gracious, slow to anger, and plenteous in mercy" . . . that "he knoweth our frame" (Psalms 103:8, 14).

All that Stan the new Christian was sure of, was that, in his own estimation, he had disqualified himself from the Christian race.

It took time and patience for the more mature Christian to help the newcomer, to reassure him that God does not give up on us; that He is the God of the special touch for the one who needs it.

I might not be able to empathize with this college boy if I had not had something of a similar experience myself.

I know that many Christians can look back on a total experience of never once having doubted God and His grace and His goodness and His fairness to us who claim to have accepted Jesus as our Saviour. It would be good to be able to say, "I never doubted God." But it wouldn't be true. My unbelief was short-lived, but it was real enough for me to enter into the feelings of those I meet who are undergoing similar problems.

For one weekend, I was ready to quit Christianity. It was a couple of months after I had quite dramatically come into contact with a Christian who captivated me with his tales of the Second Coming of Christ, a totally new area for me. I listened to the preaching of the gospel and almost immediately accepted Christ as my Saviour (although with almost no background of understanding at the time). It was my own brand of logic that nearly did my faith in. Reading the Gospels, I began to try to visualize what it must have been like to live when Jesus was on earth. Realizing that the disciples were so rarely privileged as to spend time with the living Lord, to ask Him questions, to discuss eternal things with Him; just to breathe the same air He breathed, captured my imagination and made me envious of them. They knew Jesus *personally.* They witnessed the miracles He did. *No wonder they believed! Anybody would have,* I thought, in my ignorance and naiveté. And it seemed to me that it was unfair of God to expect the same of us in our generation.

I wrestled with these feelings and with my own rationale: All I have is what I read and what other people tell me. The people of Jesus' day had the witness of their own eyes and ears.

Fortunately, I didn't keep these feelings to myself. Looking back now, I'm certain that Satan was standing on the sidelines, alternately rubbing his hands in glee and cheering me on in my confusion. Also, as I reflect on that black weekend, I can see how the Holy Spirit of God led me, even though I was questioning God in what must surely be a sinful manner. But God can stand our questionings, I have found.

It would have been the most natural thing in the world for me, when I was feeling disillusioned with the whole Christian package and I had few resources of my own to fall back on, to have sought out my old friends and shared with them what I was thinking. They would have reinforced me, I know, probably complimented me on my sagacity in recognizing how foolish I had been, before I'd gotten too far into "religion." Why I didn't go to them, I can only attribute to the loving care of the Lord. I went to the same preacher who had first interested me in the gospel of Jesus Christ, and, like Stan, I announced, "I'm giving up. I don't have what it takes to be a Christian." Then I spilled out to him what I have just explained, my feelings that, as a believer in Christ in this generation, I was being cheated of the special blessings the disciples and those who knew Jesus in Person had enjoyed.

I suspect I was not the first one who had come with such a complaint to this earnest evangelist who had been about his Father's business on a Saturday night when I first met him.

He didn't show indignation at my presumption in questioning God. He didn't ridicule me for my lack of understanding of God. He didn't laugh at me, pooh-pooh my ideas, or belittle me in any way whatsoever. He let me talk. Maybe I did this, as one man has described such emotion-packed talking, at "fifty miles an hour, sometimes gusting up to seventy." When I was finished, in quiet tones, this man explained to me something of what the disciples had to withstand in their day. But, much more significant for me at that time, he told me how the Christian message had withstood the test of time; that we had much more enduring witness than that of physical miracles. He told me of the men and women who had joyfully gone to their death because they believed and nothing could quench their belief in God and in His Son, Jesus Christ. He made me realize how much it meant to have in my hand a Bible, which the disciples did not possess in their day. So many things this man patiently went over for me, in order that I would know what was mine in Christ.

I never again felt like giving up. Oh, I had a spell of doubt that God was able to meet our needs as a family (you'll find that in another chapter of this book: "How Big Is Your God?") But I never questioned the validity, the viability of believing, in the sense of drawing comparisons between our privileges and what the first Christians had to encourage them.

That was a special thing God did for me. He met me at my point of need. He always does for His people when the question is sincere.

Undoubtedly the Lord has the spiritual welfare of our friends in mind, as well as our own, when He straightens out our confused thinking. For, no matter how new we are in the faith, there are always some who take us as examples of what a professed Christian is.

It was really something when I was converted. My friends began to lay bets as to how long I would stick with it. One week—two weeks —a month—three months? And when we met, without exception someone or more than one person would have Bible questions they expected me to answer. Amazingly, from somewhere, these answers would come. What then if I had shown up one day and announced,

"You'll be glad to know I've given up on the religious business"? If it had been just that, of course, there would have been nothing to either hang on to, or give up.

Quite recently, I heard a person say with a great deal of sadness in her voice, "I was beginning to believe in God; I really wanted to have this experience called being 'born again.' But now, the very person who stirred these longings in me has, herself, just told me to 'forget it: There's nothing to it.' I feel more empty than before."

As I listened to this disillusioned person who had been, apparently, not far from the kingdom, I thanked God anew for not letting me give up, thus possibly influencing someone adversely.

It's good to know that "The Lord knoweth them that are his," and that we are sealed with His seal (*see* 2 Timothy 2:19). We may foolishly get ourselves into confusion, but the Lord will not let Satan triumph over His purchased possession.

Not only in the matter of misconceptions or reservations about what we believe, but in a multitude of ways, God administers His special touch. All we need do to find out about the different ways is to get about fifty Christians together and turn them loose to tell of some special thing God has done in their lives. I would guarantee at least fifty instances would be shared.

Sometimes the needed touch is for bodily healing. And who can dispute that God does heal today? I have a very dear relative who is a case in point. Hers was a documented miracle case of recovery from deadly poliomyelitis. In her own words, "I knew I was dying, and, educated in a convent school, I knew the names of the saints who were in charge of various departments. But I didn't know if the patron saint of the sick would get through in time, so I went right to 'headquarters' myself." That night (on which she was to have died according to the finest medical minds on her case), God touched her with His special touch. And she has been a joy and a blessing to innumerable people ever since.

Things have changed somewhat since Christ's days on earth. While His healings drew crowds as is always true when someone is meeting human need in a spectacular fashion, nevertheless the greatest wonder was expressed not over the miracles of physical healing but the fact that people were being healed of the disease of *sin!*

"This man *forgives sins*," was both the indictment and the object of amazement. In our day, we tend to be blasé about a person's having his sins forgiven by the Lord, but to be divinely healed—that's something else!

Whatever the need, God can come with His special touch. He is sufficient no matter what the problem. Paul found that to be true for his problem: his "thorn in the flesh" (2 Corinthians 12:7). Ever since, people have been trying to ferret out just exactly what was Paul's thorn in the flesh. Suppose we knew for sure? Would that not put a limit on the help and consolation we can all take from the verses:

Three times I begged the Lord to rid me of it, but his answer was: 'My grace is all you need; power comes to its full strength in weakness.'

vs. 8,9 NEB

Paul received all the grace he needed to stand the test of whatever physical ill plagued him for the rest of his life. If we could know what it was, might we not be tempted to say at times, "Oh, but if Paul had had *my* problem, what then? Would he have felt God's grace was sufficient for him?" The inference is that, no, of course he would not have found it to be so. (We're so constituted, it seems, that each of us feels that nobody else's ills are nearly as bad as we have to bear.)

We can rest assured, however, that God has His special touch for you and for me; just what we need and when we need it. And He wants us to learn to take this from Him.

5

Oh, You Shouldn't Have

How often have you handed something to a person and had him respond with, "You shouldn't have done that."

It's not a rebuke. Rather, the person is indicating, generally, that it's too much. The response is a self-deprecating giveaway. It says, "I am not worth the money or the time or the thought you expended on me."

The manner in which we react in accepting a gift tells volumes about our self-concept.

Another "you shouldn't have" reaction comes sometimes from the very opposite type of person. Far from being self-deprecating, he is peacock proud. By his response he is saying, "You shouldn't have done this; you should have done more." His apparent humility is in reality a bid for greater recognition.

Here is a clearly developed picture of the person who has been made to feel too important, that indeed nothing is too good for him, that the world owes him a living, whether or not he ever does anything to deserve it.

Either attitude, the overly humble or the overly proud, is emotionally unhealthy. In the one, everything is "too good"; in the other, nothing is good enough. In each case the solution is found in the Word of God. The one needs to take a fresh look at what God has to offer, to make him feel worthy; the other needs to be helped to realize that, whatever he is, whatever his talents or abilities, is because of God's goodness to him. This person may indeed be unusually gifted, charming, personable, seemingly worthy of much recognition, but—the question comes to every one of us, ultimately: What do you have that you did not receive?" (*see* 1 Corinthians 4:7). Paul the Apostle had an incisive way of focusing on this truth we all need to be confronted with at some time:

> What are you so puffed up about? What do you have that God hasn't given you? And if all you have is from God, why act as though you are so great, and as though you have accomplished something on your own?
>
> 1 Corinthians 4:7 LB

However, along my way in life I have met a far greater number of the self-effacing, hangdog, "You shouldn't have" people than those who just take things and appear to think they deserve even more.

Both attitudes stem from definable roots. There are certain basics that go into the makeup of the reasonably well-adjusted person. These are not qualities which modern psychologists have either discovered or invented, though we are certainly indebted to them for emphasizing this field of thought in our day. But, long ago, these fundamental personality ingredients were clearly spelled out in the Bible. The feeling of *self-worth,* for example, is best met as we accept the worth that God gives us through Jesus Christ.

Sadly, for many a Christian, such a concept is just that, a Bible truth which somehow has never been internalized in a life-changing way. The verse, "Therefore if any man be in Christ, he is a new creature" (2 Corinthians 5:17) sounds nice to them. It's "a good verse to memorize"—but its exciting potential has somehow not grabbed them. They don't see themselves as new persons, with all that *new* holds out for them.

Some people go most or even all of their lifetimes unable to accept things from other people. This is bad enough. But the most serious aspect is that their feelings often extend to their relationship with God. They can never feel clean and forgiven and worthy.

A woman wrote to me a few weeks ago, "I can't forget my sins. Even the stick of gum I stole when I was five years old."

In this, was she, perhaps, saying, "I can't take forgiveness from God. Oh, I know the Bible says that Jesus died for all the sins of the world; He paid for *my* sins and if I ask Him, He will personalize this payment for me—but He shouldn't have done that for me. Not for *me*. I'm not worth it." Admitting she has no inner resources with which to satisfy her need to feel forgiven, she likewise demonstrates an inability to take forgiveness from the Lord. She doesn't see herself as having "forgiveness credit" with the Lord. (Strange, in a society like ours, that flourishes—practically functions—on credit.)

God does not send monthly statements, of course. He doesn't need to. He has issued, in the Bible, a perpetual credit mandate:

> If we confess our sins, he is faithful and just to forgive us our sins, and to cleanse us from all unrighteousness.
>
> i John 1:9

This credit never runs out, so long as we meet the conditions spelled out in that verse.

Interestingly, while I was writing this chapter, I received in the mail an unusual statement. It was from Bank Americard, and the instructions to me were these—spelled out in bold red capitals:

> ### PLEASE DO NOT SEND PAYMENT
> ### YOU HAVE A CREDIT BALANCE

The explanation was simple: A technical error had caused me to be overcharged earlier, and this was the correction.

It was a good feeling to know I had a credit balance. And this is exactly what each individual Christian has, in God's "bank"—a credit balance of available forgiveness. (And no computer can ever foul it up!)

So we see that it is no light thing to be unable to accept good things from other people, for this can and frequently does extend to our inability to appropriate for ourselves *God's* good gifts.

Parents can, without realizing it, instill and foster these attitudes in their children. How often I've been guilty of this myself, when my children were young. In an honest effort to have my son and daughter show what I considered sufficient appreciation, I would overdo it, have them say (if I didn't say it for them) to a person who gave them a gift, "That's too much. You really shouldn't have." So a child grows up feeling, "If it's very nice, or expensive, or if it took a long time to make, am I *worth* it?"

It could be, of course, that an individual may very honestly not be used to having nice things done for him, or receiving nice presents from people. We're not thinking of that situation at this point.

It's a fact that the person who is reasonably well balanced along these lines—neither too self-effacing nor conceited—is in the favorable position of being honestly, sincerely able to receive a gift, thank the giver, and go on to enjoy what has been given. He feels no compulsion to probe into his feelings and question himself as to whether or not he's worthy.

Such probing when carried to excess is never healthy for the emotions. In the case of a Christian it can lead to destructive introspection; beyond that, it can and does, frequently, lead to depression. I recall a case in point. It concerned a young fellow I'll call Phil, one of a big family of happy, cheerful brothers and sisters in a better-than-average Christian home. We had long been family friends and had spent lots of time together, though with varying intervals cf not seeing one another. It was after such a period that we dropped in for a visit. An unwonted gloom made itself felt. Nobody was singing in that musically talented family. The Christian *joie de vivre* was missing.

"It's our Phil," the father explained, with misery and embarrassment fighting for top place as he told us.

In brief, it was this. Phil, an earnest professing Christian who had even publicly committed his life for full-time service to Christ, had now totally changed. He was verbally *denying his own salvation.*

His mother's tearful evaluation, "It's so sudden—and for *no reason,*" made us—my preacher husband and me—wonder.

"Can you *please* talk to Phil? You know what a good Christian he's been, always ready to do anything for the Lord and to help other people. Now. . . ." It seemed neither the father or mother could bear to go on.

"You mean he's saying he never accepted Jesus as his Saviour, *that he isn't a Christian?"* We tried to clarify the issue, which didn't make even a little bit of sense to either of us, anymore than it did to the young man's family.

"That's what he's telling us," the father said, then he added, "I'm so glad you've come. Maybe the Lord sent you. Phil likes you folks. Maybe you can show him how wrong he is."

I wouldn't criticize or judge these unhappy parents for their attitude. Mine would probably have been worse in similar circumstances (until I learned better). We did seek out Phil but not to point out to him how wrong he was.

We never learned all that led to this really fine Christian's lapse from the joy of his salvation. We found him, obviously careless of his appearance and this in itself was disturbing to the parents, absorbed in deep, contemplative study of profound theological treatises. He was becoming hermitlike. To his gregarious family this spelled out that Phil had serious problems. And since, he, himself, attributed the change in his behavior to his *spiritual* state, all the parents could seem to conclude was that their son was wrong and needed to be set right.

Well, if there was anything Phil didn't need at that time it was someone telling him his thinking was wrong. As unhappy as he so obviously was, he would have changed if he could. He already felt unworthy and guilty and sinful; so far down that he would have had to reach up to touch bottom. What he needed was not someone to confirm to him how far down he was, but someone to toss him a rope, to help him out of his slimy pit of doubt.

It's a happy-ending story. Phil did regain his spiritual health and his faith. Ultimately he renewed his commitment and to this day is serving Christ. But it took time; long hours of a concerned person's being willing to listen while being nonjudgmental.

It's important for us to keep in mind that change does take time. More, it takes patience. We're so prone to dismiss a person's problems with, "He knows the Bible. Why isn't that enough? Why can't he straighten out?" If it were all that simple, many psychiatrists and psychologists and counselors could shut up shop. The preaching on Sundays would cure all the emotional ills of the churchgoers, and the others could get their therapy from the radio or TV preachers. For, whether we're prepared to admit it or not, Christians make up a part of the increasing stream steadily flowing into the professional counselor's office.

Much as I believe in Bible reading and prayer, I know many cases where reading from the Scriptures and praying with the individual has not been enough. There are times when a Christian is too emotionally befogged to (1) comprehend the liberating truth, and (2) appropriate it for himself. Somebody has, through understanding and love, to get underneath the crust. The mists of confusion, the clouds of doubt and unbelief can best be dispelled as the person is helped to appropriate Christ's unchanging love. Absorbed into his heart, this will warm and cheer like the sun breaking through the fog. And God delights to use people—you and me—to be His go-between.

There are a number of reasons why, as Christians, we should not write off the fellow Christian who has, for whatever reason, seemingly tossed away his belief.

For one thing, we can't fully know the causes. Only Jesus Christ knows our inner thoughts, knows what motivates us and causes us to do certain things. So we are guilty of judging without adequate knowledge when we presume to cast off such a person as Phil.

Second, who is more in need of our understanding and Christian love and patience? The person must be utterly miserable. For when we have lived in the light and warmth and sense of family belonging-ness that is ours in Christ, how awful must be the darkness and cold and sense of alienation of someone who, temporarily, has turned his back on God.

Still a third reason is that, usually, we do not travel that misery path alone. In the majority of instances, we drag one or more along with us. It would be characteristic of such a person as Phil not to think of himself as having any such influence on another individual. I can almost hear him saying, "Who, *me*! Nobody's watching me. My behavior doesn't affect anybody."

But this is never true. Whether we're willing to accept the responsibility or not, someone is watching. No matter how insignificant we may feel ourselves to be, almost certainly there is someone in our surroundings who feels even less important and looks to us. This is true in general terms of ability, knowledge, personal appearance, work performance, and so forth. In these areas, however, our influence does not have eternal value. But when a weaker Christian or some not-yet-Christian takes as a sample someone who then fails them by *his* abdication of his high position in Christ, this *can* have eternal ramifications.

Nevertheless, I would like to reiterate—to emphasize—that our first concern be for the unhappy Christian himself. It won't help to point out how wrong he is, or how much misery he is causing his family, or his poor testimony in the local church.

The sooner Phil and all the others in like circumstances are helped by sincere, concerned loving brothers and sisters in Christ, the less damage will be sustained to themselves, to others around them, and to the cause of Christ.

It helps, when we might be tempted to judge and be un-Christlike, to recognize that "Here, but for the grace of God, go I."

The happy consequences of demonstrated loving patience and understanding (as in the case of the man I have called *Phil*) can be a restored, fruitful Christian who emerges from his personal Slough of Despond a man of deeper faith.

Because he has had the experience of receiving what he needed from fellow Christians—Christ's representatives—he is now in a favorable situation to take things from the Lord.

And he will not be liable to feel (defensively), "Oh, You shouldn't have, Lord."

6

But You *Don't* Understand

It's a common enough scene. A friend or relative or neighbor has suffered a severe trial, the death of a loved one, or some other shattering blow. And someone comes along and says with the best intentions in the world, "I understand."

These words may come across to the sufferer with the clang of sounding brass or the shallowness of tinkling cymbal. In either case, not only do they not help, but, generally, they are a hindrance as a means of comfort.

Mary, a young wife and mother, had borne up remarkably well following the fatal car accident that snatched her little five-year-old daughter from their home. Brokenhearted, Mary yet managed to reach out to the God of all comfort and appropriate grace to help in her time of need. That is, until, some days after the funeral, a well-meaning neighbor met this bereaved mother just outside her house, and said, "I understand just what you're going through."

Mary's response astonished this neighbor. Relating the incident, she explained, "All I wanted to do was sympathize with her, poor thing. I just said, 'I understand,' and she turned on me with, 'No! You don't understand,' and then ran into her house and shut the door." With a somewhat aggrieved look, the neighbor declared, "I *don't understand* whatever made her act like that!"

What would cause a normal Christian to react as Mary did to someone whose desire was to be helpful? One reason was obvious. The neighbor didn't have any children. Her "understanding" savored of that of the happily married woman who assures a widow or divorcée, "I understand."

Also, when we use this form of condolence, seemingly the person tends to hear it as making less of the problem than it really is; it's as if we convey, "Everybody has some trouble in their lifetime. Now try to forget yours and get on with the business of living." And it's true that no matter how bitter a blow life deals us, we must somehow rally and face life again. But it helps if people close to us will let us talk about it sometimes, not putting a scab of "understanding" over the wound before it is healed and thereby causing it to fester and become a longtime sore.

A friend with whom I had discussed this subject told me about her experience when an office colleague's husband was killed in Viet Nam.

"I just went up to her and put my arm around her and said, 'You know, Betty, that I can't understand what you're going through. The Lord has never called me to suffer such a trial. But I want you to know that I love you—I care about what happens to you—and I'm praying every day for you.'

"She squeezed both my hands, thanking me for not just saying, 'I understand.' "

The bereaved woman had then opened up and talked, between the flow of healing tears. And there had been no anger.

I remember, during a period of deep trial in my own life, a day when I was poor company for other people as well as for myself. I was riding with some folks I love very much and who love me. The lady reached to where I was in the back seat and said, "I understand." Just that —and she said it gently. I still can hear my own angry retort, "No, you don't" (for I knew her circumstances and mine). How could she possibly understand?

Immediately I was angry at myself and ashamed for my ungracious and certainly unchristian response. I felt so guilty. How could I say such a thing? Why did I act as I did?

I do not feel justified for my words at that time. But I do understand to a degree what prompted them. The soothing "I understand" had in it (all unwittingly, I'm sure) the element of shush-shush with which we silence a child. But maybe the child has a need and he wants to express it, not be shushed. I could not have articulated it at the time, but now I realize that I didn't want to hear, "I understand" (with its close-the-door or its change-the-subject connotation). I needed someone to say at that time, "Is something troubling you? Would you like to talk about it?" When this was not forthcoming, the result was anger: anger at myself; a strong feeling of guilt. Certainly it was not the result intended by the kind person who said, "I understand."

It may be, however, that the person is really signaling that he has enough troubles of his own. He can't handle his own and yours, too. So it's easier to say, "I understand," perhaps trusting that this will close out the discussion.

We can only understand with true empathy what we have personally experienced. The mother who has stood over a tiny casket is in a strategic position to say to one who is undergoing such a trial, "I understand."

Some years ago we received a phone call from a distraught young doctor telling us their baby—just hours old—had died, and asking that I would go and visit his wife. They were new Christians and I recognized that this could be a blow to their faith as well as being heartbreaking. But what could I say to this young mother whose arms were aching from emptiness? Nothing in my own experience gave me anything viable to say to her. Oh, I could read and quote from the Bible; I could pray with her. And these are both relevant and powerful at such times. But would they reach her in this hour of need? To my mind came another family to whom this same tragedy had come a year or so earlier. I asked this lovely young woman if she would go with me and she willingly consented, taking along with her some reading matter that had particularly helped her. Although it reopened her own wounds, she shared with the girl whose baby had just died the very things that had comforted her in the same situation. There was no "Just take it from the Lord" brush-off; rather, together we took the grief and the burden and the questions and the sorrow *to* the Lord, the great Comforter.

Sometimes a person who has suffered deeply shrinks from entering into another's present grief. They may not want to reopen wounds.

"I'm just getting over it," they may say, "and I don't want to bring it all back."

They don't want to uncover the layers that time has spun over their sorrow. We would not judge them for this. But, by so doing, they may withhold from someone who desperately needs it, the greatest of all human therapy, genuine, empathetic understanding.

Moreover, if we are Christians, we have a mandate to share comfort:

> What a wonderful God we have . . . the one who so wonderfully comforts and strengthens us in our hardships and trials. And why does he do this? So that when others are troubled, needing our sympathy and encouragement, we can pass on to them this same help and comfort God has given us.
>
> 2 Corinthians 1:3,4 LB

Am I saying, then, that unless I have suffered the loss of a loved one, I should not attempt to speak words of consolation to someone who is bereaved?

If I have not known bitter disappointment and disillusionment, I would do better to keep quiet in the presence of one who is so suffering?

No. We should all be comforters, but with sincerity and honesty. By admitting that we do not understand but we *care,* we may even cause the stricken person to feel, "Here is someone who really understands."

Nor is it inappropriate to say that you *have* gone through certain trials; but it's best not to elaborate on your own. This may cause the person whom you wish to comfort to get the impression that you think one trial is as great as another. This can completely defeat your purpose. It will come through as an emotional put-down. This is especially true when one person says to the other, "Just take this trial as from the Lord."

Fortunately for humanity there are innumerable instances when people do understand. They have "sat where we sit" (*see* Ezekiel 3:15). They have had trials similar to our own and when they reach out with comfort, there is reality in it. Also, once in a while we come across a person who, though he may not necessarily have suffered a great deal, appears to have remarkable insight into other people's problems and need for understanding.

Perhaps we rob ourselves and other people whom we could help, by not availing ourselves of the wisdom God promises. "If any of you lack wisdom, let him ask of God," the Scripture tells us (James 1:5).

We're not Solomons. But, as believers in and followers of Jesus Christ, we can have understanding hearts. (It has always intrigued me that, of all the options open to him, Solomon asked God to give him an *understanding heart!*)

Ultimately, however, for total understanding we must go to the Lord.

The disciples knew this. Grieved over the untimely death of John the Baptist, "They went and told Jesus" (*see* Matthew 14:12). On another occasion, Peter said poignantly, "Lord, to whom shall we go?" (John 6:68).

Jesus has sat where we sit—whatever our sorrow. He is the Man of sorrows. He is acquainted with grief. What a comfort it is to know that:

> There's not a pang that rends the heart,
> But God in heaven shares a part.

Jesus will never offer less than the comfort we need. He will never give the wrong kind of comfort. He has no stock phrases or clichés such as we, in our human ineptness, sometimes latch onto and dispense as "comfort."

Jesus alone wholly understands us as individuals with distinctly different needs. He has no prepackaged comfort marked *A, B,* or *C,* to suit general categories of need. He knows how to so work in our hearts and lives that we can take whatever He sends into our lives "as from the Lord."

We have another plus going for us as Christians, to help us understand and be understanding. We have a *built-in Comforter.*

If ever a group of people needed comfort, it was the disconsolate disciples when Jesus told them He was going to leave them. But He did not leave them comfortless. And He told them so. In the days and

years that followed, in every circumstance and trial, it was the Holy
Spirit, the Comforter, who made it possible for the disciples to take
whatever happened to them as from the Lord, to see His purpose in
it, and to comfort one another.

You and I can appropriate what is rightfully ours as Christians. We
can live in the consciousness that the Holy Spirit indwells us. In turn
we ourselves can be comforters. We may not always understand another person's problem. But we can be supportive and encouraging
and help that person to take things as from the Lord. He understands.

7

The God of Your Circumstances

We ask, "How are you?" and the reply comes, "Oh, all right—under the circumstances."

This answer can be just a convenient conversational cliché rather than an admission that the person is "under his circumstances." Frequently, however, it means what it says.

For us as Christians to be avowedly under our circumstances is to be denying that God is our heavenly Father, that He is love, that He does care for His people.

Not that we bypass the ills that afflct all mankind, believer and unbeliever alike. But, convinced that God has a plan for our lives (my personal, basic philosophy), we know and feel that He is the God of our circumstances. This belief has a profound bearing on one's ability to "take things from the Lord."

Such assurance doesn't come all at once. There's no fishpond we can dip into and pull out a package which, when we open it, will provide us with lifetime, unassailable faith and the ability to stay on top of our circumstances. No. This balance-producing emotional stability comes from faith that has been put into practice. ". . . prove me," God challenges (Malachi 3:10). God can stand our test. We cannot figuratively stand on the sidelines watching other people proving God and thereby grow strong in faith ourselves.

Sometimes a homey little situation teaches us an important lesson. Did you ever bite into a kumquat, that tiny, shiny, pebble-skinned, elongated miniature orange? My introduction to it was memorable as an example of what I've been saying.

I had picked a couple of kumquats from the tree and was admiring their perfection of appearance when some people standing nearby said, "Try one." Their eagerness for my reaction should have alerted me that the tasty looking morsel was not all it seemed. I nibbled gingerly, then screwed up my face and protested, "It's *sour!*" (If I had been alone I would have spat it out.)

"Keep eating it," urged the friends who were obviously enjoying themselves at my expense. They added, "It'll turn sweet." I wasn't buying that—till I noticed the encouraging nod from a woman who, I knew, would not urge me for the sake of seeing me squirm. So I popped the rest of the kumquat into my mouth and as I chewed it, I discovered that the folks were right. That sour-as-lemons fruit turned into the sweetest, most refreshing thing I had tasted in a long time. Now, when they are in season, I deliberately seek out that tree and help myself to sweetness and refreshment. Yes, the first bite is still something to be gotten over in a hurry. But I believe and know it will become sweetness—and it does.

I could have gone the rest of my life believing that my friends undoubtedly knew what they were talking about. But if I had never really tried it for myself, I would not have known for sure that the bitter-skinned kumquat is filled with sweetness on the inside.

In similar ways, the things that God sends our way may not always be sweet to our taste at first. It may be, at times, something we would like to spit out. But if we can just bring ourselves to believe that it is from the Lord, therefore it is good and good for us, it will become "as honey for sweetness" to quote Ezekiel (3:3).

I was reminded that day and I have been many times since that God can and does turn the bitter into sweet. So I've learned to take things from the Lord. Sometimes they have been, indeed, bitter at first. But as I've trusted my heavenly Father instead of "spitting it out," in incredible ways that would fill a volume, He has worked in the circumstances, sweetening things for me.

Some Christians admit that they hesitate to be open with God to the point of saying with honesty, "Thy will be done." They fear to do this lest they might encounter difficulties. (I constantly marvel at how distrustful most of us are, how fixed our assumption that a new experience will be bad rather than its having a fifty-fifty chance of being good.)

We would hesitate to come right out and say, "If it's from the Lord, it's likely to be unpalatable." Yet, honesty might reveal that such is at least part of our thinking. I have heard people say, "If I yield my will to the Lord, I'm afraid He'll send me off to some jungle to serve Him." And God may do just that. He does send some who serve Him into the world's jungles. Jesus did say, "So send I you," and there was no geographic boundary indicated. But we can be sure that when we are *God*-sent, that jungle will be the safest and the happiest and most productive place we could possibly be. In the same context, the person who fears to trust his life to Christ may find that the place he has chosen in preference to God's will for his life is much more of a "jungle."

Not infrequently, when a person speaks of being "under the circumstances," he is referring to economic insecurity. This area likewise enters into our thinking with respect to honestly seeking God's will. "If I tell God I want His will for my life, He may ask me to live on practically nothing" (again, the presumption of the worst!). These attitudes don't do much for God, in respect to public relations.

It does happen that God calls some people to live on a low economic level. I know about that, for our first assignment was a home-missions charge, and for many Christians there seems to be little reason to regard home missions in the same light as foreign, with the result that not too much support is assigned to the home area. But, as I found, happiness has little to do with a paycheck. I look back on those days as some of the most joy-filled of my life. To be sure, friends from our home church rather pitied us. And they verbally wondered about a man who had proven himself a supersalesman. "You could sell glasses to a blind man and refrigerators to the Eskimos," they would tell my husband—and the inference was clear. Some well-intentioned people would go a step further: "It's all right for you. But what about your children, your bright, intelligent son and daughter? You'll never be able to send them to college." That would have been bitter—but did God let it happen? No. I don't know where the faith came from, but I can remember saying again and again, "If we're faithful right now, doing what we believe to be God's will, even though we can't be setting aside a college fund, when the time comes God will provide. And He did, abundantly. The Lord makes "college grants" as well as every other kind of provision, if we will only trust Him to do what is best for us.

I think we would have difficulty in finding many of God's committed servants—especially foreign missionaries—who would agree that they are "poor" (even though a tax consultant did say to my daughter, Jeannie, "My dear, your salary is under the poverty level"). Nor have I heard any complain of being "under the circumstances" and mean it. God has His ways of bringing sweetness into the most seemingly bitter circumstance. That is because He is the God of our circumstances.

A little thought about the word *circumstance* should tell us (without our digging into its roots) what it means. The *circum* part immediately speaks of circle. And that's an important factor in any generation, any culture or socioeconomic bracket. To be in the right circle is all-important. Many times this is the *entrée,* the open sesame to some desirable function or experience from which we would otherwise be excluded. And who feels good about being an outsider? It's not only that we are denied whatever the experience would give us; but our ego is also attacked. We feel that not only are we lacking in credentials, but that we ourselves do not measure up. So it's a secure feeling to know that one is in the right circles.

Then the *stance*: that's easy to interpret, also. The stance is our position; where we stand. A politician is often asked by his constituents to "define his stance" on certain important issues. By his reply he raises certain expectations and these can have a strong influence on his candidacy when election time rolls around.

Put together, the *circum* and the *stance* is the position in the circle (the surroundings) in which we find ourselves. It speaks of a set of externals and what we let them do to us and in us and through us.

Doesn't it make your blood course a little faster when you remember and realize that, as Christians, we are "in Christ"; that our life is "hid with Christ in God" (Colossians 3:3)? We are encircled, enveloped by His love and care. *That* should keep us rejoicing, keep us from being under any circumstance. Agreed?

It occurs to me that we can demonstrate selfishness or unselfishness by the way we react to what life sends our way. I've heard some people say, "It's my own business how I behave." Maybe it is and maybe it isn't. No man is an island. As Paul phrases this, "For none of us liveth to himself, and none dieth to himself" (Romans 14:7 ASV). What we do, how we react to circumstances, influences those around us. They see us as being under or on top of our circumstances.

Some of the most quietly influential Christian witnesses in the world are those who can take their circumstances as from the Lord and live above them. Their secret? Whether they have sat down and reasoned it all through, which I doubt in the case of the ones I know personally, they have a realization that they are in the right circle. They are *in Christ.* (The Pauline epistles are a great study as to what we are "in Christ Jesus.")

I have a friend who has been sightless all of her life. She accepts her blindness, and her radiant love for Christ spills over to everybody she meets. "She makes God look good," a Brooklyn bus driver said of my friend, Gladys. In turn, Gladys has the idea that the whole world is love—and lovely. "All I have to do is step outside my door," she tells me, "and a whole lot of people begin to show concern for me. I always have more people willing to help me than I really need when I'm downtown shopping, or finding my way to places." She is one of God's best ads. One doesn't need seeing eyes, apparently, to have a radiant smile and an overflowing friendliness toward other people. Gladys is, as far as I have observed, never *under* her circumstances; never selfishly absorbed with her own problems. In a manner that is not pious, not sticky sentimental, she talks about "my wonderful Lord." And she's believable.

When the opposite is true, how detrimental it can be to the cause of Christ, as the non-Christian develops a mind-set against belieivng in the Lord.

A funeral director I've known for some years is virtually impossible to reach with the gospel. His rationale or excuse or whatever he intends to present to God at the end of his life is this: "For twenty years, in the course of my duties, I've attended funeral services. I hear what the minister is saying. But I observe how his parishioners and others behave. And this confuses me. If, as I've heard innumerable times, dying is better than living, why do the people who profess to have faith in God act as though there's no tomorrow for any of them. You'd think *God* had died, to watch and listen to some of them!"

In the irrational way in which the unbeliever views anything spiritual, it doesn't occur to this undertaker that the people he is so judging are human and acting like human beings; that their behavior is no way invalidates Christianity, making it "phony" as he frequently describes the Christian faith. To be fair, we must assume that he is judging the forest by some little trees. While he has seen some Christians go to pieces at the funeral of one they loved, he must also have viewed equally as many whose calm, quiet trust in God upheld them. Let me say here that I would certainly never crusade for tearless funerals. It is God who gave us our emotions and He surely doesn't mean that we should repress these emotions in the presence of grief. Our Lord, Himself, wept at the grave of one He loved. (I would hope *some* will cry when I die!) But we should be able to sorrow as those who have hope—and faith in the God of Easter.

Because we are all different, we can be expected to react differently. Many things in life contribute to our ability to withstand difficulties and problems. Who can tell what has fed into the background of a person, causing him to act and react as he does? Take the case of two women, each of whom loses her husband through death. Their situation and circumstances prior to this bereavement appear to parallel each other's. But one woman rides the rough wave, seemingly buoyed up all through the trauma. The other behaves in a totally different manner: She's rebellious against God and her circumstances; she cannot be consoled by her friends. In fact she almost resents their implication that there is consolation for her.

"I don't understand," people said. "Both Joan and Alice love the Lord. Why should Joan be able to accept her husband's death as she's doing, while Alice, who claims to be a mature Christian, has gone all to pieces and is bitter aginst the Lord?" The friends shook their heads over the seeming paradox. If these friends could have looked at the early formative years of each of these women, they might have found some reasons why Joan had a reserve of security that Alice almost totally lacked. As long as both were sailing the smooth seas of having a husband to depend upon, to provide them with love and attention and material necessities, one woman seemed as secure as the other. But when the storms of life came, one had a bulwark of inner security and the other did not. Consequently, one was "under the circumstances," and the other on top.

For many—Christian and non-Christian—this area of our emotions, more than material deprivation, finds us under our circumstances. Depression heads the list, for no one is free of depression 100 percent of the time. That should be encouraging. It was to me when I first heard it. So prevalent is depression to one degree or another, that psychiatrists and psychologists have dubbed it "the common cold" of emotional ills. If a permanent cure could be discovered, many of them could take down their shingle (so I've heard a number of them say). Many things can trigger depression: the loss of a loved one, severe disappointment, a business failure—anything that would knock the props from under us. Surely, then, we can recognize the wisdom of having a firm foundation on which to rest our faith and hope for today and tomorrow.

For some people, because they are basically emotionally healthy, the feelings of depression are short-lived. They can get on top of their circumstances. Like David the psalmist they may realize that, yes, they are cast down. David was, apparently, frequently downcast in spirit (see Psalms 42, 43). But while he admitted to having such feelings he knew where to go for help.

Why art thou cast down, O my soul? . . . hope in God. . . .

Psalms 43:5

(The person who is habitually depressed probably needs professional help, and, thank God, this is increasingly available in a Christian setting. Nor is there the stigma which formerly attached itself to an admission of an emotional or mental problem. No one need go through life suffering from debilitating depression.)

The antidote always readily available to the believer in Jesus is Paul's counsel, "Rejoice in the Lord" (Philippians 4:4). It's impossible to rejoice in what the Lord *is* and what He has done for us, and still be a prey to despair.

The key is "in the Lord": suppose we had been exhorted to rejoice in good health—or in the weather—or in prosperity or in success—or in our friends! How unpredictable one's state of health! The weather blows hot and cold. Prosperity can be fleeting, success relative. And even the best of friends can prove fickle. So "Rejoice in the Lord," we are told. He alone changes not. Jesus Christ is the same yesterday, today, and forever. Of no one and nothing else on Planet Earth can this be said.

We are encircled by this Lord in whom we can rejoice. As one of my favorite hymns assures us,

> In heavenly love abiding,
> No change my heart shall fear;
> And safe is such confiding,
> For nothing changes here. . . .

The hymn goes on to say, "God is round about me. . . ." That being so, God being round about us, nothing can touch us without its first having touched Him. We can, then, in the strictest sense of the words, take our circumstances as from the Lord. Far from being *under,* we can rejoice in the Lord and triumph over the circumstances!

The prophet Habakkuk makes a classic point of his trust in the Lord:

> Although the fig tree shall not blossom, neither shall fruit be in the vines; the labour of the olive shall fail, and the fields shall yield no meat [food]; the flock shall be cut off from the fold, and there shall be no herd in the stalls. . . .

Habakkuk 3:17

What is Habakkuk saying? Even though there's neither fruit nor grain nor wool nor meat nor oil—basics for survival—"Yet . . . I will joy in the God of my salvation" (Habakkuk 3:18).

Here is practical trust in the God of your circumstances.

It has nothing to do with the gross national product (GNP) that we hear much about in our day. The GNP of this prophet's time would have caused many of us to despair. Habakkuk could have been pardoned for being under the circumstances. But he wasn't. And he has left us the best of all reasons to put our trust in the God who is above every circumstance.

8

Does God Have Favorites?

We think of ourselves as being part of the church of God—and rightly so. But in a more personal sense we are a part of the family of God. And in families, whether we like to admit it or not, there tend to be favorites. I know some families where one child will say to a brother or sister, *"You* ask Daddy. He won't say *no* to you. You're his *favorite."*

Does our heavenly Father have favorites? Does this explain why some people easily, almost casually take things from the Lord, while others find it difficult to do so?

Some people think God does have favorites, regardless of Peter's declaration:

Most certainly *and* thoroughly I now perceive *and* understand that God shows no partiality *and* is no respecter of persons.

ACTS 10:34 AMPLIFIED

A friend of mine, a Bible-taught, wisdom-filled Christian highly regarded by people who know her, states in the most matter-of-fact tones, "I'm just one of God's spoiled children." Usually this is a wrap-up sentence when she has just shared some very special thing that God has done for her.

Her statement, "I'm one of God's spoiled children," is freqnently met with some slightly envious wonder, as though those around her felt she had a particular *in* with God, that she is indeed one of God's favorites, and that such is out of reach for them. The "favorite" has seemingly never felt any compulsion to explain. She just smiles her quiet, secure smile.

I've listened to her "spoiled child" talk, too, and I've found myself analyzing it. Hers is no quippy little remark. She isn't that kind of person. She doesn't use idle words. She appears to have arrived at the place in her spiritual maturity where she knows the Lord, trusts Him wholly, and feels completely secure in Him. It's as though she lived by the maxim. ". . . no good thing will he withhold from them that walk uprightly," and that is right out of the Psalms of David (84:11)!

Believe me, there's nothing she can't take from the Lord, be it good or be it adverse.

The slightly disturbing factor, to me, in what this Christian is saying (perhaps involuntarily propagating) is the "spoiled" concept. If I read human nature rightly I'm led to think that people do not do things *happily* for spoiled people—children or adults. We may give in to them, let them manipulate us, and thus gain favors from us. But it irritates us that we are being so used. We have a different reaction toward a *favored* child.

I really believe that what my friend is saying is, "I'm one of God's *much loved* children." And she has no corner on that market. No one need eye her as though he would fain he counted among God's spoiled children.

God does not have spoiled children. It would be out of character for Him. The Scripture is quite explicit in that we read that *because* we are His children, when we are out of line, God chastises us—in love (*see* Hebrews 12:6).

Sometimes we speak of spoiling our children: "She's so adorable," or "She's such a *good* little child that you can't help spoiling her." We don't really mean *spoil*: that's a negative quality. Rather, we're generally speaking of how much we delight in showering love and affection and attention on such a child. This child surely does feel special. But, often, he or she gives as much or more in return.

Some children do become brattish from a parent's overindulgence. Others, seemingly, can't be spoiled. I know a boy who from infancy had love and attention and gifts in abundance. He was a silver-spoon child. People delighted in him. Even strangers would stop to speak to him in his carriage, and he would smile and wave at one and all, like royalty on a parade route. But all the attention and all the presents he received did not develop spoiled-child traits in him. He responded with a delight that made other people feel happy. There was no question about it. This little boy *was* a favorite.

What makes for favoritism? Why does a parent single out one child in the family and shower everything on him? Other factors can enter in, but, from my observation, people reach out to the one—even a child—who meets some need of their own. We all have inner needs. And some children and young people give love to a parent to a marked degree. A strong bond is formed—and sometimes it comes across to others, even other family members, as favoritism toward the child.

Does God have favorites? Special saints He singles out for His particular favors? It would appear so. Some, both Old Testament and New, seemingly have special status with God. Abraham was one who did. God shared His secrets with Abraham (*see* Genesis 12:1–3; 13:14–18; 15:1–18:33), and we only do this with a person in whom we feel complete confidence. Abraham had made God supreme in his own life. God could trust Abraham.

Moses likewise enjoyed a unique relationship with God in his generation. Moses led a fantastic life as a result of his "Choosing rather to suffer affliction with the people of God, than to enjoy the pleasures of sin for a season" (Hebrews 11:25). For this he gained an unchallenged place in history as the emancipator of his people.

Then there is David, the beloved shepherd king, the "sweet singer of Israel" (*see* 2 Samuel 23:1). With his gifts, we might speculate to what heights he would have attained in the literary world of his day. But how impoverished the world would have been through the centuries without his masterpiece, the Twenty-Third Psalm! This and all of David's writing sprang from the deep well of a heart that found its satisfaction in his God in good times and in bad. David delighted himself in the Lord his God—and God delighted Himself in David, "a man after his own heart" (1 Samuel 13:14).

We might dwell on others: Noah, Joshua, Elijah, to name just a few who were mightily favored by God. And what of the disciples, twelve men who walked and talked with the Son of God for three years, and

Mary and Martha who had the inestimable privilege of having *Jesus* stop by at their house for a rest and a meal? And Paul the Apostle? Surely he was one of God's favorites! But far outstripping all of them, it was a woman who was most highly favored: Mary, the mother of Jesus. She was a favorite—and she knew it. ". . . all generations shall call me blessed" (Luke 1:48), she said. She was right, for they have called her blessed. Like the others whom we have mentioned, Mary delighted herself in the Lord. The timeless *Magnificat* (Luke 1:46-55) begins:

> My soul doth magnify the Lord, And my spirit hath rejoiced in God my Saviour. . . .

> Luke 1:46, 47

Even Mary needed a Saviour and she was quick to admit it. Indeed not any of the favorites we've been dealing with were sinless or perfect. Abraham, often called "The father of the faithful," had a great lapse of faith that threatened to endanger both himself and his beautiful wife (*see* Genesis 20).

Moses, "the meekest man who ever lived," displayed anger which so displeased the Lord that Moses missed out on entering the promised land (Numbers 20:7-12).

David, "the man after God's own heart," committed gross sin (2 Samuel 11:1-17).

Despite their sins and weaknesses of the flesh, however, these men and women had one vital thing going for them: they put God first to a marked degree, in everything they did. For this, God singled them out and honored them. And God is still doing the same in our day, as He has in every generation. God has His special people today—and the world is marking them as His. Some are preaching to multitudes; others are serving humanity in the name of Christ. Not all of God's heroes are unsung (although many are). Every age needs its heroes. We have to have someone to look up to. That's how God made us.

Whatever the realm, the sports world, the world of politics, or art or religion, the common denominator of greatness is one word: *dedi-*

cation. No matter what the talents or qualities, the magic key is single-eyed, one-track-mind dedication.

A friend of mine, then a new Christian, looked up the word *dedication* for fine shades of meaning. He was greatly elated to find in one dictionary this definition: ". . . as of David Livingstone"—dedication defined in terms of God's great missionary explorer in Africa. There was something prophetic in this convert's findings, for the searcher was none other than Viggo B. Olsen, M.D., the noted and much loved missionary surgeon: "Daktar" of Bangladesh. The day came when he, himself, was cited by the *New York Times* "as in the tradition of David Livingstone."

You may be thinking, *That's just great—for him, and all the other outstanding Christians I hear and read about. But me? I must have been behind the door when the talents were being handed out. I have no special gifts or abilities. I'm not one of God's favorites.*

If you feel this way (and who doesn't at some time?) I would recommend your turning in your Bible to John, chapter 15. Read verse 16: "Ye have not chosen me, but I have chosen you. . . ." Chosen. Selected. Favored by God. My own introduction to this verse came with all the startling impact of a revelation (which it was) from God. It was as though He had sent me a personal spacegram.

It was the morning after my conversion from nominal Protestantism to faith in Jesus Christ as my personal Saviour. At the suggestion of a new friend who gave me her own Bible to help implement her suggestion, I was starting this new life by reading the Bible first thing in the morning. I opened the Bible "cold"—I had almost no Bible knowledge so I wasn't looking for anything in particular—when my eyes lit on that verse, John 15:16—the words seemed to pop out at me. I gasped as I repeated to myself, "You have not chosen me, but I have chosen you." *It's true. That's me, for sure,* I thought. *I had not been seeking for God, electing to know Him and to serve Him.* Nevertheless, ever since that Monday morning in August a number of years ago, I've felt a kind of specialness. Jesus Christ Himself chose me—and He told me so in His Word. I didn't know then, and I know little more now, about the theological implications and ramifications that perplex greater minds than mine with reference to John 15:16. I just knew that

Christ chose me as a member of His family *and for a purpose.* That's enough to make anyone feel like a favorite!

In God's family we all start out even. What we become is largely up to the individual. The Holy Spirit is ours without measure, to enable us to be what God wants us to be. (It has interested me for some time that we have no biblical code we call the Do Attitudes; we do revere the Beatitudes.) *Be* attitudes. I believe that God is infinitely more concerned with what we *are* than with what we *do.* It should logically follow, of course, that when we are what God wants us to *be,* we will likely strive to *do* what He wants us to do. An advertisement we're seeing these days for a particular brand of vitamins has as its catch line, "Be *everything* you can be." That's what God is looking for, men and women who, in the context of our Christian life and witness, will be everything we can be, for Him. When we do, we will not have to worry about whether or not we are among God's favorites.

Certain privileges go with being a favorite. Possibly the most important benefit is the security we feel in the love of the One to whom we are a favorite. We have an inner assurance that when we ask for something, our request will be listened to and heeded; not be summarily dismissed or arbitrarily refused.

Some Christians would dispute the fact that God hears and answers prayer. I frequently hear, "I don't know why some people seem to have such good experiences with God. He never seems to send these things my way. I don't think He hears my prayers." And almost always, there's longing in the person's voice and a yearning look in his eyes. Yet, no one who knows Jesus as his Saviour ever need feel left out, like the proverbial stepchild. God doesn't have stepchildren. We need to keep in mind, however, that we are told to ask *in the name of Jesus,* and when we do, this will have a bearing on what we ask for. If we are going to ask in Jesus' name, we had better be asking for something Jesus would ask for. We cannot use His name and violate His character. (To return to our family analogy: we would not ask Daddy's favorite to ask *for us,* something this child would not be liable to ask apart from the nonfavorite's request.)

In this connection, recently I inadvertently overheard a part of a conversation that I could hardly believe. One person was saying to another, "Surely one of these days God will answer my prayer and give me just *the perfect squelch* for that woman!" Uh-uh! God is not in the perfect-squelch business. The person praying that prayer had best not hold his breath waiting for an answer. That is one prayer we could never pray "in the name of Jesus." A prayer God would speedily answer in such a circumstance might be, "Lord, You know how frustrating this situation is. Please give me Your grace to put up with it and be what You would have me to be." Such a prayer often is its own answer, bringing a serenity of spirit and an increase of patience and tolerance. Moreover, God will undoubtedly answer by working as only He can, on both ends of the situation. But perfect squelch? Forget it.

As members of God's family through faith in Jesus Christ, we all have access to Him. In a unique sense, though, the person who delights in God and lives close to Him has an open line to heaven and is a recipient of God's special favor.

In the human family, the favorites tend to reflect something of the one with whom they are a favorite. A small boy imitates his daddy, sometimes in his walk, or in his desire to wear the same kind of clothes his dad wears; in a number of ways this can be observed. The same is true of a little girl. In her desire to please her mother who loves her so much, she mimics her. And those who are God's favorites begin to pattern their life and their behavior so that it and they will please God.

As we said earlier, being a favorite with God has nothing to do with being a spoiled child. It means being a recipient of God's favors, as a member of His family. Having accepted His initial, eternal favor—*salvation*—they have then chosen to put themselves in the position of becoming favorites. They have delighted themselves in the Lord and, true to His promise (Psalms 37:4), God is giving them the desires of their hearts. And that's not hard to take from God! This, then, is the kind of favorites God has. You can be His favorite. I can be His favorite, beginning this very day.

Our new relationship to God will soon evidence itself to people around us. So don't be surprised if someone comes to you and says,

"Will you please pray for me? I have a need and you seem to have some kind of *in* with God."

Far from having someone else "ask Father" for us, we ourselves will be able to be a blessing to a newer or weaker brother or sister. Along the way we can also encourage others in God's family to get in on the joys and privileges of being one of God's favorites. For we can conclude that *yes,* God does have favorites.

9

How Big Is Your God?

One of the inspiring hymns of our day has a couple of lines that speak volumes. After asking the question, How big is God? the writer replies,

> He's big enough to rule the mighty universe
> And small enough to live within my heart.

Isaiah the prophet verbalized something of the same concept long ago, speaking of the One who inhabits eternity, who lives in the high and holy place, yet dwells also in the heart of the humble (*see* Isaiah 57:15). Both concepts are heartwarming and bring much security. I'm thinking particularly of the first, the greatness of God; the height and depth and all the other dimensions we would never be able to fathom as to how big God is. I am inclined to think that our ability to take things from the Lord may be predicated on our concept of this inexhaustible heavenly Father.

How big is God? The answer has to be relative. For how big you have found God is not necessarily the same as how big I have proven God to be in my life. I'm confident that God is always big enough to meet our need, but what experiences do we have along that line? I've had my own share of finding out how great God is.

I remember an experience in the early days of our ministry. And this time I'm not thinking of the wonderful, bracing, beautiful north country of Canada (as in another chapter). No. This was a city pastorate in the days of depression—recession, call it what we will—with its long lines of dispirited men looking for a job, and equally disheartened wives waiting for the good news that seldom came with the husband's arrival home.

Time and time again God came through and showed us how big He is, how abundantly able to meet our every need. And yet, I recall the day when I was really down; my faith had hit bottom. That's when you know if you have faith or not. I found that mine was a small, shallow supply. I would have asserted until then that I had strong faith in God and in His ability to meet my needs. But I discovered I did *not* have such faith.

I hang my head even now as I think of it, for there came a weekend when, because of my almost total discouragement and failure to trust Him, the Lord God taught me the lesson of a lifetime. He didn't "take me to the woodshed" as Dr. Vernon McGee picturesquely describes some of God's dealings with His children. Rather, God overwhelmed me with His goodness. He knows how best to teach each of us.

Our cupboard would have made Mother Hubbard's look well-stocked that Saturday morning—and there was no money for food. (Let me hasten to say here that our congregation was thoughtful and kind, and we shared our bad times and our good times together. But so few were employed.) These were strategic days for a compassionate pastor to just "be there" with his unfailing cheerfulness, optimism, and faith that helped many a family to hang onto both their faith and their hope for better days. Usually I was right in there, too. But that Saturday my faith had reached rock bottom. I was questioning God: "Why, if You really love us, do you let us be so poor? All I'm asking is for enough to feed our baby girl and our little boy and some for ourselves. Is that too much for You, God?"

And God showed me how big He is.

With nothing but a cup of tea, my husband had gone to an early prayer meeting (after bringing me some tea, in bed). A number of duties kept him busy until noontime, and when he arrived home I didn't have to say, "Surprise, surprise!" The aroma of pot roast greeted him. I was just starting to explain that a wonderful Russian friend in our congregation had come to the door with a basket containing the makings of a good dinner, and had told me, "The Lord especially spoke to my wife and me to do this today," when there was a knock at our door. There stood a delivery boy from a bakery, in his arms three or four boxes. We demurred about accepting the goodies but he insisted they were for us, and all paid for. It seems to me in retrospect that this was a plus the Lord sent to His servant who was *not* doubting Him, for my husband dearly loved the things that many people drool over in bakery-shop windows.

We were about to sit down to our meal when again there was an interruption. It was another delivery boy, this time with a hamper he could scarcely span with his two arms, and loaded with groceries. We knew it just had to be a mistake, so we sent him, nicely, on his way. But soon he was back and this time he was insistent: "It's for you. It was all ordered and paid for this morning." (Months later, quite coincidentally we learned the name of the family God had used to send this bounty to us.)

By this time the truth was beginning to bear in on me. I was inwardly looking for a hole to crawl into and pull the hole in after me. I felt like saying to God, "I get Your message. I know You are able and willing to supply our needs—I know You love us." I did say to Him, "Please forgive me for ever doubting You."

Some time ago I read a poignant line that has stuck with me although I cannot remember who wrote it. It was this: "What has God ever done to His children that we don't *trust* Him?"

What has God done? He has loved us and saved us from our sin and promised to meet our every need—and that's just the beginning of all He has done and will continue to do for us.

I learned something of this foundation truth that weekend in Hamilton, Ontario, so long ago. For God had not finished giving me my lesson. Making a social call on friends who were not church people, we found the husband ill. And, with God's timing, a delivery man brought *their* groceries while we were there (those were the days when stores gave such services!). These friends hadn't a notion that our finances were nil. We would never have let them know of our need, for that might have reflected on our church folk. I don't think I realized how much more it would have reflected on our Lord. Since the husband was sick, his wife suggested quite casually that maybe we could help them out and take some of their week's supply of food.

There were unexpected gifts of money that day, also, from persons who had no way of knowing that this was a crucial need at that particular time.

What a Sunday we had! A sermon on Jehovah-jireh—the Lord will provide (*see* Genesis 22:14). And a sharing of our abundance with those whose needs were great and whose cupboards were lean.

But God was not through teaching me yet. On Monday morning a neighbor who owned a corner store in our block came and with much apologizing said, "I hope you folk didn't have to go without meat for your Sunday dinner. I just found out that this package was delivered for you on Saturday night. Someone else took it from the delivery man but forgot to tell me about it. It's been in my refrigerator all weekend." So, even when we were not home to receive it, God had been showering more blessings on us.

There it was—more meat than our family could or would eat in two weeks. So again we were able to parcel it out to other families and tell them where it came from. Along the way the Lord gave me the grace to tell some people, to whom it was a spiritual blessing, of my own failure and of God's unchanging love and forgiveness.

Since that long ago weekend, I can't think of a time when I ever felt that God could not or would not care for my needs. He hasn't always given me all I've asked for, but He has been my Jehovah-jireh. He has provided for my needs, for:

> Out of His infinite riches in Jesus,
> He giveth and giveth and giveth again.

Are you, perhaps, thinking, *But that was a number of years ago.* Or, *But that was in Canada: there were people whom God could speak to, whose ears were tuned and they obeyed the inner Voice. Also the goods were available so long as the money was forthcoming.* And inherent in your reasoning is the question as to whether God is doing such specific things—meeting His children's needs—*today* and in other countries.

How big is God to the foreign missionary in an isolated jungle when the supplies are running low?

Again, I need only reflect on a personal experience for an answer to this question.

It was New Year's Eve in a missionary's home on the banks of the Matamahari River in (then) East Pakistan. Dinner was over. The kerosene lamps had been lit and we were settling down for an evening of enjoying each other—the missionaries and the stateside visitors—when there was a sound of footsteps, then a knock on the door. Our host, Harry Goehring (now present with the Lord) excused himself and we heard some discussion in a language I could not understand. Harry reappeared, beckoning us to follow him. "I think it'll take all of us," he said with a grin, and we picked our way down the steep riverbank. There, gently rocking under the moonlight, were two boats with their polemen standing alongside the bank. Swiftly the men unloaded bags and cartons and all of us pitched in to carry them up to the house. It was quite unforgettable. I helped to stack on the kitchen floor of that bamboo house cans of meat, fruit, vegetables, coffee, and other commodities. Sacks of flour and rice added to the windfall. We paused and united in giving thanks to the Giver of every good gift, the God who *still* has His ravens.

It was a miracle that American food in abundance should so unexpectedly appear at that jungle station named Hebron on a New Year's Eve! A miracle, yes, to the wondering and grateful missionaries, my own daughter among them. For this was the time of year when, as I had observed just a day or so earlier, there was almost nothing but radishes and squash to be gotten in the village markets. And the missionaries' barrels were fast becoming empty. I thought that night and I still think, that somewhere, off in another time zone, some earnest Christian had been praying, "God bless the missionaries at Hebron and supply their every need." Perhaps all the more *because* it was the New Year's season, Christians were praying for those who were sacrificing the joys of family get-togethers and all the holiday fare.

I have to confess that I used to be a little cynical of what appears to be a very general type of praying. I've even quipped, "God would have to be God to answer a prayer so unspecific as 'God bless the missionaries.' " But God *is* God. He knows our needs and He knows the needs of His servants in the far-off places; and He will bless the fervent prayer even when the one praying does not know the particular need of the moment.

How did He answer this "someone's" prayer? Ah! That's a story of God's omnipresence!

How big is God? He is big enough and knowledgeable enough and everything-else-enough to piece together a need and a source of supply in ways that would make a fiction writer hesitate to submit it to an editor (for fiction has to be more believable than truth).

During the fall of that year, a survey party from the Forestry Division of the University of Georgia had arrived in East Pakistan (now Bangladesh) to do research in the bamboo forests of that area. One day, on the painfully slow trip upriver on the country boats, a minimum of eight hours, often in sweltering heat, they had spied two houses high on the riverbank. Recognizing that these were not quite like the homes of the nationals, their curiousity was aroused. They left their boats and trekked up to investigate. Not only did they find Americans, but to their unbounded delight they found a fellow University of Georgia man (the late Reverend Harry Goehring) and his major had been forestry, until he heard God's call to work with men rather than trees. With rapport instantly established, the survey party often stopped at Hebron, and when their business took them to the port city of Chittagong, they worshiped with the missionaries on Sundays. As one of these forestry men expressed it to me personally, "Chittagong would be a dark place but for the missionaries."

Their mission accomplished, the surveyors discovered that they had overestimated their stay and had thus overbought supplies. With the option of returning the surplus to the supplier, they chose rather to donate it to their friends, the American missionaries. And I was privileged to see this answer to prayer. I saw that God is big enough, if the need arises, to transport the answer from the United States to a little country half a world away.

God does have His "ravens" to feed His Elijahs. Sometimes they fly, sometimes they come in little boats. He is Jehovah-jireh.

There's nothing special about me that God would so privilege me to be a witness to His unique provision for His own, or to personally experience these faith-enhancing happenings. Certainly I never deliberately set out any more than most Christians do to find out how big God is. Like many others, I had a kind of belief that He could meet my needs. I frequently quoted Philippians 4:19, ". . . my God shall supply all your need . . ." but that was it—until God unmistakably showed me.

For most Christians, God's provision is not a neon-lights thing. It's more often demonstrated in His everyday faithfulness, His mercies that are new every morning, God keeping His promise. But for some, like me, because we obviously need to have it made very real and very plain to us, God does the spectacular. We can then pass on to others who need such assurance, how big God is.

It doesn't take any great achievement for God to do the overabundant for any of us. He threw the stars into place and these eons later no man can explain how He did it. God's "bigness" showed before the world was. Creation was a series of all-time *firsts*. Since then and in particular after the birth, life, death, Resurrection, and Ascension of His Son, Jesus Christ, the spectacular things God has been doing are the quiet things in the hearts of those who love Him. In the true sense, you and I will find that God is as big as we will let Him be.

Not always is it in material things that we need to have God do big things for us. Often, our emotional needs more often cry out for fulfillment. This, too, we can learn to take from the Lord. But that's another chapter.

10

The Original Defense Mechanism

Two preschoolers were playing when one stumbled and fell down. He began to cry, and when his mother came to console him, he howled, "It was Joey's fault. He pushed me." It happened that the mother knew better. She had seen what occurred, and Joey was in no way to blame.

Tossing blame. Childish? Yes, but not confined to childhood.

One student copies from another, and when he is confronted with his cheating, he turns and blames the other fellow. "If he hadn't had his paper where I could see it, I wouldn't have copied from it."

We're probably all guilty at some time of looking around to find someone whom we can blame for something that is our own fault.

Where did it all begin? In the *beginning*.

The world was very young when this defense mechanism—blaming another person in order to escape the consequences of our own sin—was first used. Adam needed a way out, if he was going to appear in the right light before God. (As though any maneuvering would fool the Almighty!) So Adam, when he was questioned by God about whether or not he had eaten fruit from the forbidden tree, was quick to defend himself.

"Yes," Adam admitted, "but it was the woman you gave me who brought me some, and I ate it."

Genesis 3:12 LB

It's as though Adam was saying to God, "If You had never brought her to me, if Eve had never appeared on the scene, I would not have been tempted. Don't blame me." In so saying, Adam would have, in effect, been saying, "It's Your fault, God. You are to blame."

> Then the Lord God asked the woman, "How could you do such a thing?"
>
> V. 13

Eve was quick to catch on, with her husband as her model.

> "The serpent tricked me," she replied.
>
> V. 13

Adam blamed his wife (and God). Eve blamed the serpent. Ever since, man has used this defense mechanism of blame as an excuse for a variety of behaviors. We have the example of our first parents. But why is little said of the consequences to their own family, apart from what has affected all mankind?

Have you considered that the first murderer was Adam and Eve's son (possibly a teen-ager)? His victim, their only other child! Daily headlines have somewhat inured us to horrors but we still feel particular revulsion when the homocide is brother against brother or child against his parents. And we should!

Not only blaming and murder, but jealousy, envy, callousness, and lying have a long history. In fact, the "works of the flesh" as recorded in Galatians 5, at least in part, could have made the headlines in Century One. Hear the insolent murderer, Cain: God asks him, "Where is Abel, thy brother?" Cain's reply? "I know not: Am I my brother's keeper?" (Genesis 4:9). (And we hear it said that ours is the most incorrigible generation of young people who ever lived!)

Eve believed the devil's lie. She opened Pandora's box and its contents have plagued humanity ever since. One way we have sought to cope with problems of our own making has been to blame somebody else.

But blame is a poor way of covering up our failings and shortcomings. How much better to confess, "I did it." There's great self-help in being honest. You feel a better person. You haven't used the crutch of blame. You've stood on your own two feet.

Blame can have irrevocable effects on the person who is wrongly accused. But, apart from that important consideration, when you don't stoop to blame another for your faults, you stand taller yourself.

Nevertheless, we are largely a race of buck-passers (a notable exception being the late President Truman who reputedly had in his office in the White House a plaque that read, THE BUCK STOPS HERE).

In our practice of projecting blame we have even extended it to God in His heaven.

"The Lord did it to me," we complain in our childish whine (until we learn better), and this attitude colors some people's ability to take things from the Lord.

Let's think about this matter of blaming God. It really doesn't make sense, does it? If we love someone and profess to believe that the someone also loves us, don't we want to put the person in the very best light before other people? Blaming God for what happens to us isn't the best way to portray our God as what He is, for God *is* love —and loving. It's a sad commentary on that love when we keep blaming God for various things in life.

There is, of course, a sense in which God *lets* us do things to ourselves. He could stop us if the thing is detrimental to us in any way. But God will not violate the free will He Himself has bestowed on human beings, the attribute that lifts us above all other living creatures. Our ability to make choices is God-given. We are stewards of this gift and will one day have to give account of our stewardship. But God will never "break our will"; never force us to do His will.

When we fail to heed the inner voice—call it conscience or, in the Christian, the Holy Spirit—we must accept responsibility for the consequences. This in no way gives us the right to blame God.

Blaming others doesn't relieve us of feelings of guilt. We subconsciously know it's not the right thing to do. Paul the Apostle had the right idea when he said, "For I know that in me (that is, in my flesh,) dwelleth no good thing" (Romans 7:18). Paul could have given very good excuses for his sins (of persecuting the Christians, for example). He could have blamed his rigorous religious training. Zaccheus the tax collector had a ready out if he had wished to defend his practices. He could have blamed the Romans who hired him and made it easy for him to collect a percentage for himself.

In tossing blame at other people, not only are we being unfair and perhaps harming them, we are not helping ourselves or improving our own emotional well-being.

There is something therapeutic in being able to recognize when we are in the wrong and then in doing something about it. Not that we need to beat ourselves over the head, saying "I'm such a terrible person," or "Only a stupid person like me would do such a thing." Not at all. What I have in mind is that we do ourselves a favor when we acknowledge that we have either done something we should not have done, or we've left undone something for which we are responsible. It shouldn't pose any great problem to admit this, and, where another is involved, to go to that person and say, "I did this, and I'm sorry." This clears the air and we both feel better.

When we do not acknowledge our fault but rather blame someone else, we assume an emotional debt to that person. We have placed on him a burden for which we ourselves are responsible. It's hard to have any kind of good relationship with someone to whom we owe a debt. (Perhaps that's why Shakespeare said, "Neither a borrower nor a lender be.") And in Romans 13:8 we read, "Owe no man any thing, but to love one another."

When the debt is an emotional matter, such as when we have wronged the person, how high the interest! It builds and builds. But there is a way to be rid of it. It's as simple, many times, as saying, "I'm sorry. Please forgive me."

I can't buy Erich Segal's *Love Story* line: "Love is never having to say, 'I'm sorry.' "

At first hearing, this seems a beautiful, idealistic, almost Sermon-on-the-Mount sentiment: something to accept and practice. But it really doesn't stand investigating as a practical measure for good relationships. If we never say, *I'm sorry,* we stunt our own emotional growth. And that's not the only consequence. Carried to its logical conclusion this "never having to say, 'I'm sorry' " can become a rationale, a justification for all kinds of behavior. It could lead to such thinking as, *Why worry about what I do or say? People will understand. Those who love me will never expect me to be sorry. I won't have to apologize for my actions or my words.*

Far from love's being justification for our not saying, *I'm sorry,* it would be more realistic to describe love as *being willing* to say, *I'm sorry.*

Furthermore, we are not, most of us, emotionally constituted to be able to take, on a long-term basis, conduct that calls for a *sorry,* which is never expressed. A genuine sign of love would occur when we create a climate wherein the other person and we ourselves can say, *I'm sorry,*—and be accepted. On the contrary, when we figuratively push away the *sorry,* we're shutting off not only communication on the matter, but the person himself. Can this be love?

It may sound like a good deal. But it's not. It's *not true.* The Bible is quite specific in that we should confess our faults one to another (James 5:16). Note, the word is *faults.* We confess our *sins* to *God* alone. When we have confessed our faults, as the verse goes on to say, the happy result is that we then pray for each other. There isn't much communion between us, or between us and God, when some problem stands in the way. We find it hard to approach the person we have wrongly blamed for something. And God seems a million light-years away. It takes the honest confession to restore the relationship, and sweet fellowship results in our praying for each other. Actually, I question that we *can* pray for each other if some unconfessed wrong is not dealt with. The healing comes and the communication channels are reopened to each other and to heaven when we do things God's way. We had best forget Erich Segal's Jenny and her theory of what love is.

It's not an easy thing to ask for forgiveness, to say, *I'm sorry.* But the person we do not, or feel we cannot, forgive, will haunt our prayer life. Jesus said this would happen. Remember when He said,

'If, when you are bringing your gift to the altar, you suddenly remember that your brother has a grievance against you, leave your gift where it is before the altar. First go and make your peace with your brother, and only then come back and offer your gift.'

                                                    Matthew 5:23, 24 NEB

In this instance that Jesus cites, it's the one who feels someone has something against him, who makes the move for reconciliation. The principle applies in either case. Our devotional life is affected if the channels of forgiveness get blocked from either end. I can recall some time ago when I thought I could never, never forgive a certain person who, I felt, had grievously wronged me. I knew this was keeping me from the warm, close fellowship with Christ that makes life so worth living. I did pray about the situation. I did confess to the Lord what my problem was and I did ask Him to help me overcome it, for it wasn't a good feeling. Every time I knelt to pray it was as if a sheet dropped between myself and God. All unbidden this person would come into my mind. But God knew my heart and when I really came to the place where I didn't care who was to blame just so the situation could be cleared up as far as I was concerned, God began to work. It was not possible for me to go to, or even to communicate with, the person who was invading my prayer life. But the Lord *changed me.* It was not an all-at-once thing. But I distinctly remember the day when, down on my knees, I sincerely prayed for this one whom I had not been able to either pray for or forget. A completely new joy overwhelmed me. This was a spiritual victory and I knew it. I felt healed of a worrisome sore. And it has never returned.

Even when we have wronged *God* by blaming Him for things, it pays to confess this wrong. You may have been thinking, *God, You don't love me anymore; You're not answering my prayer; all kinds of bad things are happening to me and where are You, God?* In this, you're blaming the Lord for deserting you; for failing you. That calls for confession.

It's a healthy thing to admit when we're wrong, even to God who knows anyway. There's healing of the spirit as we speak it out, hear ourselves saying the words and asking forgiveness. Then we can accept the wonderful freedom that comes from feeling forgiven. It's a whole new start.

The fact is that when we throw the blame for something we did onto someone else, we still have to live with ourselves. Other people may see us as guiltless, but we find it hard to forgive ourselves. Haven't you found that the hardest person to be at odds with is yourself? I have. So it's good to get things off our chests by honest confession.

It's interesting that the maxim, "Confession is good for the soul," is not found in the Bible. Yet many people quote it with all the authority of Scripture.

Confession is also good for the emotions. And it's a mark of emotional, as well as spiritual, maturity when we have grown up sufficiently to be able to confess when confession is in order.

Blame-throwing is for little children, until they learn a better way to cope.

Accepting responsibility is for grown-ups.

We categorize ourselves by how we assume due responsibility for our failings and shortcomings.

Why play the blame game?

Why blame *God?*

11

Getting In on a Good Thing

One of the most forthright statements in the Bible is: "It is a good thing to give thanks unto the Lord" (Psalms 92:1).

We appear to have an innate sense that this verse is true. We see this in our training of children. One of the earliest phrases we labor to get a child to say is *thank you.*

"Say thank you, Mary, say thank you." And the mother with a degree of anxiety in her voice asks, "Did she say thank you?" then turning to the child she will reiterate, "Did you say thank you to the lady?"

Why is it so important? To be sure there are instances when the mother makes much of such things in order to appear in a good light herself: "Look at me. I'm bringing up my child right." But what makes saying *thank you* such a big, important part of it? Because, in the heart of us we know that it's a good thing to give thanks, to have a thankful spirit.

Those of us who have been drilled from infancy to say thank you may have to take our thankful spirit out and look at it once in a while; examine ourselves as to our heart attitude as grateful souls.

Left to themselves, children will generally be crystal clear along this line. Think of a Christmas scene, for instance. Billy's fingers are all thumbs as he struggles excitedly with the wrappings on a package. He finally tears aside the tissue and uncovers the gift. The next few seconds can often reveal more about his parents and his training than they do Billy's own feelings and appreciation of the gift. He may react in one of two ways if the gift does not meet his Christmas expectations. With the donor of the gift (perhaps his grandmother or another relative) and his anxious parents' eyes on him, he may mutter a *thank you* and just look his disappointment.

The child to whom saying thank you has not been made a ritual may speak and act exactly as he feels. He may blurt out, "Not pajamas!" or "Oh, that's the *second* one of these I've got," and hurry on to the next package.

We're not, of course, advocating that a child be permitted to be rude or insensitive to the fact that a person who has made him a gift should be treated nicely. But how often when a rigid, "Be sure you say thank you" is programmed into him, the child will grow up with little sense of what it means to feel thankful and to express it from his heart.

Another short, crisp sentence in the Bible is, "In everything give thanks." We can skip lightly over it. Or this verse, as we internalize and practice it, can help keep us on an even keel emotionally. It's instruction loaded with therapeutic value.

Having a thankful spirit is not only good, it is one of the best things in the world; it brings the rewards of obedience, for the Bible says unequivocally that we should give thanks.

No one is born feeling thankful. We're grasping, demanding, thankless little creatures. We have to learn to give thanks, and some people who never seem to learn are ultimately social misfits.

Giving thanks to the Lord has broad ramifications: deep implications and practical applications. When we give thanks to God for everything that happens to us, we are in fact placing the responsibility for our welfare squarely on God's shoulders. This is "taking it from the Lord," in the strictest sense of the term. Such an attitude of heart causes us to look for God's hand in our circumstances. And how much resistance and resentment that forestalls. We can take as good and perfect everything God sends our way; good and perfect because of the Source, not because the thing is necessarily either good or perfect, in our opinion, at the time.

Just a few days ago I saw this principle in action. A man knocked on my office door and as I saw who he was, I was at a loss for the right thing to say, for his lovely wife had died just two weeks earlier. They were one of God's beautiful couples, with everything to live for and a tremendous involvement with people, witnessing for Christ. I was deeply moved for I had loved this woman very much. I'll never forget the grieving husband's greeting to me. With his right hand upraised, he said, "Praise the Lord!"

This was "in everything giving thanks." Not a what-else-can-I-do gesture of hopeless resignation. It was, rather, an acknowledgement that *God* was at the heart of the dire circumstance, and, built into his "Praise the Lord" was the affirmation that God would see him through.

The practice of giving thanks can revolutionize our lives. It's not that God needs our thanks in order to be happy. But He did create us for fellowship with Himself, for His pleasure. Surely it ought to be a two-way relationship; not God doing all the giving. (That would savor of the couple who have a joint bank account. The husband says, "I put it in and my wife takes it out.") For everything God "puts in our account," the only thing we can give in return is our thankful selves.

One of the practical benefits of cultivating a spirit of thankfulness is that gratitude and griping cannot coexist. Think of the emotional fringe benefits there! A thankful spirit can prevent frown lines in one's face, while a prolonged whining spirit almost inevitably reveals itself in the person's face.

To further underscore the emotional bonus of being thankful and taking things from the Lord, here is another New Testament nugget:

> Don't worry about anything; instead, pray about everything; tell God your needs and don't forget to thank him for his answers. . . . His peace will keep your thoughts and your hearts quiet and at rest. . . .
>
> Philippians 4:6, 7 LB

A thankful spirit is both a preventative and an antidote to anxiety. No wonder we're reading and hearing about increasing numbers of the medical profession investigating this concept! We are a worry-ridden, anxiety-prone society (and with good reason in many instances). But every generation has had cause to be anxious, every era breeds its own fears—and the timeless counsel of God is, "Don't worry." This is not some ethereal word potion for the irresponsible; not a formula to ease our own conscience while we leave the burdens for someone else to shoulder. It is, for the Christian in particular, a common-sense approach to problems. As we take the trial as from the Lord who loves us, and thank Him in everything (not necessarily *for* everything), we free our minds to be objective. Frequently this results in our seeing a creative solution. I see this as the combination which Paul recommends, prayer and thanksgiving. Tuning into God in this way releases His power in us and enhances our ability to think through a situation clearly and deal with it creatively.

An instance comes to my mind. My daughter, a missionary in Bangladesh, was just winding up her furlough. At the same time she was taking graduate studies and preparing for her return to her work overseas. She was almost inundated with things to do. Much of the work she had to do herself because of its character, but she welcomed help for a number of areas. One evening a small group of friends came. Before their arrival, she organized particular tasks, then, taking a large piece of poster board, she listed the various things. Across the top, in banner letters, she wrote, **JOB OPPORTUNITIES.**

I can see those women even now in my mind's eye. They immediately spotted the prominently displayed poster. Job opportunities! Intrigued, they scanned the list and each one selected an "opportunity" for herself. They could hardly wait to get our buffet dinner over, so they could tackle these jobs. And an amazing dent was made that evening in the "to do" list.

Without this creative approach the evening might have been a drag. What if my daughter had greeted her helpers with a deep sigh and said, "I'm glad to see you—but there's *so* much to do I hardly know where to begin!" She didn't. She thanked the Lord for both the load of work and for the helpful friends who were willing to step in and be extra hands when she needed them.

When we have a thankful spirit we keep finding things to be thankful for all day long, and this habitual attitude brightens and lightens the day.

It's also a mark of maturity to be thankful. As babies we are gimme-gimme persons. As baby Christians we have to be taught to develop a spirit of thankfulness to God. When we do, we are on the way to spiritual maturity, which in turn is a major factor in emotional maturity. The individual who has traded childish resentment and resistance against God for trust and acceptance of his situation experiences a feeling of well-being that the thankless person can never know.

Of all people, we in the Western world have more than anyone else for which to be thankful to God. Just a few minutes of honest contemplation on God's goodness to us should effectively puncture any gloom balloon that's depressing us.

A thankful spirit is a viable witness to the practical power of God in the daily life of a believer in Christ. I remember reading of a woman whose radiant faith and consistent spirit of thankfulness had earned her the loving nomenclature, Thanksgiving Anne.

In our present-day Christian community we sometimes see PTL on a lapel pin or a bumper sticker. The initials were not immediately meaningful to me, but I learned that they stand for "Praise The Lord." It's a good thing to praise the Lord whatever means we employ (as long as we are sincere and our life bears out our other expressions of praise to God).

Our first and ultimate cause for thanksgiving to God is that, as Christians, we belong to Him. This truth in the final analysis takes care of us for both time and eternity. We can take what He chooses to send our way, knowing that for us, trials and troubles and problems will all be over one day; that a new day will dawn; as a hymnist phrases it, "a day without a cloud." The mere prospect should flood us with thanksgiving.

It should follow that when we are thankful to God we will be likewise thankful to people. But this is not always so. In Christian circles as in every other, some people are more mature than others, so we do well not to be judgmental if not every Christian we meet has a thankful spirit.

Then, time and again I keep hearing, "This is surely the most thankless generation that ever lived!" Doesn't it seem a bit presumptuous for people to make pronouncements that involve generations in which they themselves have not lived, so they can't possibly be in a position to evaluate truly?

All too often the indictment is directed at our young people, justly or unjustly. As a group, young people are both thankful and unthankful; we can't lump them all together and label them ingrates. It may be that some who are obviously unthankful in their attitudes are displaying a brand of honesty. They refuse to say *thank you* for things they didn't ask for and would never have chosen. Generally the reference is to material things. Are they, in not expressing gratitude for such things, crying out their hunger for the things which are not seen and can't be handled, the abstracts: love, understanding, appreciation, the things that give us good feelings? Gifts that we don't want do not make us feel good. And the honesty of some of our young people has them saying,

"Why should I say thank you? I didn't want it. It was thrust on me. Maybe it makes you feel good to give it. But it doesn't make me feel good to receive it."

We may deplore both the words and the attitude they express; instead, we might do well to try to understand the young person.

Sometimes we hear that thankfulness is going out of style; that, apart from trotting it out once a year—November if you're American; October if you're Canadian, and so on—"nobody's thankful anymore."

The Apostle Paul gave us a clue we can believe better than modern man's theories. Writing to Timothy, Paul explicitly pinpointed unthankfulness as one of the marks of the last days.

This know also, that in the last days perilous times shall come. For men shall be . . . disobedient to parents, unthankful, unholy.

2 Timothy 3:1, 2

There are mounting scriptural signs that this could be the generation that will see the Second Coming of Jesus Christ—earthquakes where they have never before been reported, famines, knowledge explosion, spiritual phenomena, among other signs. To these can be added the spirit of unthankfulness that is abroad on the earth.

Many people say as they consider their circumstances, "Why

should I be thankful?" There are plenty of reasons. Even the ability to raise the question is a gift from God.

The Bible makes much of thankfulness, not chiefly for the sake of the other person but because it is good for us ourselves.

Nevertheless, we do become distressed to one degree or another at the ingratitude of someone we care enough about to give a gift. It seems to me that the reason for it is that we like to think the very best of people we love and—let me say it again—we feel innately that thankfulness is a good thing, that a thankful spirit is a mark of a good person.

It may go further than that in our feelings. It could be that when, habitually, thanks is withheld, the giver feels that his gift is treated lightly or even rejected. Consequently he, because he cares for the person, feels that not only his gift but he himself is lightly esteemed or even rejected. Haven't you heard perhaps a grandparent say, "I sent my grandson a gift, but I never heard if he got it"?

A woman said to me in this connection, "Maybe my friend is signaling that she doesn't want anything to do with me anymore." There's a world of sadness in such instances.

Parents, grandparents and others agonize over what Shakespeare describes as:

> How sharper than a serpent's tooth it is
> To have a thankless child.

What, then, must our heavenly Father feel when we, His children, constantly exhibit a spirit of unthankfulness? But perhaps to the greatest degree we rob ourselves of a good thing.

The Bible never uses idle or misleading words. When we read, "It is a good thing to give thanks to the Lord," we'd better believe it— and get in on this good thing!

12

But Why, God?

A mother sighs, "If I only knew why he does it!" and she launches into an explanation or a defence of her son's inappropriate behavior.

An employer says in some exasperation, "If I could think of a reason for the way my secretary acts!"

A wife laments to herself, "Why would Tom ever do such a thing?"

Every day, in hundreds of situations, people are asking, Why?

Built into this questioning is, "I could take it, if I just understood why it has to be." Furthermore, the person is inferring, "Why does it have to happen to me?"

I have questioned in this way myself; I don't know one person who has ever talked over a problem with me, who has not intimated that the why of it perplexed him.

Most of all, we question God. This is the eternal why: Why does God let it happen? God does not have to answer. He is not obligated to explain to His creatures. This truth is clearly taught in Romans 9:20 AMPLIFIED:

> But who are you, a mere man, to criticize *and* contradict *and* answer back to God? Will what is formed say to him that formed it, Why have you made me thus?

> [Also *see* Isaiah 28:16;45:9.]

We can dwell on the questioning and when we do this unduly, this is in itself a form of unwillingness to take what God sends our way.

And such rebellion can create feelings of guilt that only compound the problem.

An alternative reaction open to us is not to question God but, as Job was enabled to say, "Though he slay me, yet will I trust in him" (13:15).

We can help each other find peace in the midst of trials, through our nonquestioning attitude: our Job-like trust.

One of my dearest friends taught me this. Her husband, a minister, was stricken with a severe and long illness. His work for the Lord ground to a halt; the house had to be kept hushed; no visitors, few telephone calls—and months when the prospects that he would recover from the necessary surgery were dim indeed.

During those long months (knowing what my own reactions would probably have been in the same circumstances) my friend was a walking question mark to me (and to others). She remained calm and trusting. Later, when the Lord had graciously restored her husband to health and he was again active in his church, we talked about the difficult days. I asked what had kept her going.

Very thoughtfully, my friend said, "It was George himself. I saw how he was taking this severe trial. Never once did he question the Lord's will in the matter. Never did I hear him say, 'Why would God let this happen?' or 'Why me, God?' And because he was able to take it—all the pain and the inactivity and the uncertainty of any cure— I was able to take it. And, again and again I seemed to hear God saying to me, 'Be still and know that I am God.' "

My friend could take it because God could trust her husband to take the trial as from Him.

This was a new concept to me—and what a tremendous insight it brought: that one person's ability to accept what God sends can be predicated upon the reaction of another Christian when trouble comes. This told me that we can do things when we have the right model to pattern ourselves after.

What happens when we do *take it?*

This can lead to creative acceptance. And a classic example comes to my mind. God's work was flourishing at the Memorial Christian Hospital in Malumghat, East Pakistan (now Bangladesh), when, beginning with the wife of the medical director, Dr. Viggo Olsen, their daughter, and my daughter, a nurse in that hospital, a form of hepatitis mowed down the staff. I recall the day I heard that Dr. Olsen had sent a cable to his mission board in Philadelphia, saying, "I am ordering the hospital closed and I am ordering myself to bed."

Close a mission hospital? Who ever heard of doing such a thing? In fact, when Dr. Olsen ordered my daughter, Jeannie, to leave the Outpatient Department of which she was the director, and "go hang up your uniform and get to bed," she retorted, "That's ridiculous! How can I 'go to bed'?" But she did—for seven months.

Did things grind to a halt? Yes. For a brief period the hospital was closed. The disease defied the efforts of even a research team (who arrived) to categorize it. But during the long seige that affected every missionary family and a number of the national hospital staff, many long-delayed projects got underway. Theirs was not the stillness of stagnation.

Dr. Olsen describes those days, in the book *Daktar,* after outlining nineteen important areas that had been accomplished only because of the epidemic:

> Ultimately it dawned on us why God "cranked out" a new disease, unknown to medical science, with a remarkably high attack rate, and symptoms which stopped our normal activities for many weeks, yet allowed us to accomplish huge amounts of sedentary work. Our Father knew that we could not rightfully, in good conscience, close the hospital to accomplish other urgent work even if such a thought had occurred to us. But God took the initiative and *set the priorities Himself!* Apparently some work or works among the nineteen were of such high importance that a drastic rearrangement of our schedule was warranted.

When we can see God's hand in the trial and take the situation as from Him, we are freed to act creatively. In the Bangladesh instance, the literature ministry which my daughter heads up got its launching and is, today, the most important *Bengali* language source of Christian reading material in the country of eighty million people.

Back to my friend and her Bible verse. "Be still"—sometimes the only thing God asks of us is that we keep a calm frame of mind, which in itself contributes greatly to our ability to take things. It may be difficult for some of us to keep still, but God does not issue mandates without giving us the inner resources for being still—we restless, querulous creatures.

"And know that I am God." Here is where the strength lies, in the knowledge that God *is,* and that He is for us.

So we can be calm and take what God wills.

Unwittingly, some well-meaning people make it harder for us to take the trial and remain reasonable and accepting of it.

Take the case of Jim and Joan. Joan came home from her teaching job seething at what she called "the way they're treating me." She raved about unfairness on the part of the administration, about favoritism and rank-pulling and "every trick in the book." Her anger was triggered by a promotion that she had hoped for being given to another teacher in her school.

"They can't do that and get away with it," her husband, Jim, exclaimed. The more he empathized with her, the greater her hostility grew. Everyone was wrong, and out to beat her out of her due recognition.

What if, as a Christian, and with his wife's true welfare at heart, Jim had listened without necessarily agreeing with Joan's point of view of the situation? If he had guided the conversation in such a way that Joan could see that there were other opportunities she might have; other promotions; that this was not the end of her world and that the Lord might have something much better in store for her?

As it was, this teacher never progressed to personal maturity from that time on. She grew warped, suspicious, vindictive. And her own uninviting attitudes kept her from future possible promotions. She developed a sour disposition as a direct result of not being able to take what life dealt her that one day. Had she looked further than her colleagues and seen God's hand in what happened, who knows how far she might have gone in her profession? But, her life stunted and herself unhappy, God could not use her as He would otherwise have done.

It's hard to accept disappointments in life. But how we react at such times shouts aloud what we really are on the inside. And how often, when taken in the right spirit, disappointments have proven to be God's appointments.

Sometimes we're doing all right until "help" comes. Especially difficult "Job's comforters" are those who have all the answers. They "know why" the particular trial has come upon us. And their implied inside knowledge (sometimes finger-pointing) adds to the woes. We might question: Does God, when He veils from the afflicted person His reason, His divine purpose, then reveal it to a friend or acquaintance of the sufferer? Is this not presumptuous thinking on the part of the friend who professes to "know why"?

God does use people in our lives, to help us, but they are not generally the "I know" kind.

One of the most afflicted of human beings was the man noted for his inspiring and lovely hymn, "It Is Well With My Soul," Horatio Spafford.

We might think that surely sunshiny circumstances led to such assurance as "It is well, it is well with my soul."

It was in the city of Jerusalem I heard the story of this hymn from the lips of the author's own daughter, then a woman in her eighties, Mrs. Bertha Spafford Vester.

Shortly after the Chicago Fire, the Spafford family had opened their home to many refugees and evacuees from the city and Mrs. Spafford had spent her strength ministering to them. For refreshing, her husband arranged for her to take their four little daughters and travel to Europe where he would join her as soon as his business permitted. But the ship on which they sailed, the French liner S.S. *Ville du Havre,* sank as the result of a collision and Mrs. Spafford's tragic cable to her husband read, "Saved alone."

On his voyage across the Atlantic to join his wife, Horatio Spafford was called into the private cabin of the captain, who said, "A careful reckoning has been made, and I believe we are now passing the place where the *Ville du Havre* was wrecked."

"To Father," said Mrs. Vester, "this was a 'passing through the valley of the shadow of death,' but his faith came through triumphant and strong. On the high seas near where his children had perished, he wrote,

> When peace, like a river, attendeth my way . . .
> It is well, it is well, with my soul.

The Spaffords had not seen the end of tragedy, however. The only son born to them died of scarlet fever when he was two and a half years old. Added to the grief was the attitude of some Christians who surrounded them. It was popularly believed that God sent sorrow as retribution for sin. So, following the drowning of four daughters and the death of their only son, the question was being raised, "What has this family done that God is so afflicting them?"

And there were those who "knew why."

This made the tragedy all the more difficult to live with, even though, earlier, Mr. Spafford had said, "I am glad to trust the Lord when it will cost me something."

There are still people who are just as judgmental and cruel as to take it upon themselves to say, "I know why God has sent this trial into your life."

A Christian couple had separated and there seemed to be little prospect of reconciliation. A fellow Christian said to the wife, "I know why God has sent this into your life. He wants to do something very special for you and this is His way of doing it."

In vain did the woman protest, "I can't believe that God causes one Christian to fall into gross sin (in this case, adultery) just so He can do some work in my life. I can't think that this is how God works."

We do well, when we're in the presence of some other Christian who is undergoing some trial, either to keep quiet and sincerely pray for him, or else offer some words of assurance, not probing why or presuming to know why. There are generally enough *whys* in the person's own mind, without the rest of us adding a few, or planting seeds of doubt as to God's love in His dealings with the person—doubts that might make it hard for him to take it from the Lord.

I don't think God works that way. God does not always tell us why, but He gives us the assurance that "He knows the way I take" and we can be sure of His ultimate purpose (*see* Job 23:10).

I know a man who suffered a severe heart attack. An evangelist, well-meaning, undoubtedly, visited the sick man. Pounding on the bed, the evangelist prayed that God would reveal the sin that was the cause of the man's seizure: that the man would confess and repent and that God would then heal him. The man's wife explained that even in the midst of the trial, the Lord was precious to them. She told that they had been having hard times financially and that, as a result of her husband's illness, people had paid them money long owed, and that in other ways, the Lord was wonderfully meeting all their needs. To which the preacher replied almost scathingly, "I'd hate to think my Father had to knock me down to feed me." God's provision did not fit into the evangelist's assessment of the situation, that the sickness was the result of some sin in the man's life.

It pays to let God be God. He knows the whys. That's enough to keep us trusting Him, come what may.

There is an ultimate *why* that should engage our minds. It is, "Why does God so love us? *Why* did God so love the world that He gave His only begotten Son, that whosoever believes in Him should not perish but have everlasting life?"

This is the reasonable eternal *why*—the question of the ages!

The "Why me, God?" is another whole area of questioning. Why, when so many Christians seem to be sailing smooth seas, should others be called on to face storms and trials?

Early in my own Christian life, this paradox bothered me. It didn't help one bit when I heard something that just didn't make a bit of sense to me. Some Christians were talking about a certain family in the church. "God must be able to trust them very much; He's sent so much sorrow their way," I heard these people say. Not only so, but the way they said it sounded as though this were some special kind

of reward God was handing out to this family—like for faithfulness.
I couldn't understand that. It was as if the computer that is my finite
brain (finite, but still more sophisticated and complex than the most
awesome that man can invent), were rejecting and tossing out such
thinking as "wrong information." In my ignorance of God's Word I
had never heard that God's thoughts are not my thoughts, nor my
ways His ways; that God said, ". . . as the heavens are higher than
the earth, so are . . . my thoughts than your thoughts" (Isaiah 55:9).
But I was to learn that God knows best what to use for building blocks
for character and spiritual maturity, and that we just rob ourselves
with our petulant questioning, "Why *me,* God? Why don't You shove
this trial off on somebody else?"

I'm aware of the verses in Hebrews chapter 12 that tell of God's
dealings with His children. But I have a theory—and it's just a theory
of my own that I would like to submit. It seems to me that when God
assigns some trouble area to us, He then lovingly watches to see our
stress level, how much we can bear. And accordingly He entrusts us
with ever heavier burdens.

The clue to doing this is, of course, that not only do we take the
trial as from the Lord, but we likewise *take the grace to bear it* which
comes with every trial or sorrow. We never get the one without the
other, unless we, ourselves, refuse to accept God's always offered
resources of help in time of trouble.

God is our refuge and strength, a very present help in trouble.

Psalms 46:1

It's as we take the trial as from the Lord and act accordingly in the
midst of it, that we become (as my friend was to me) a living question
mark. People ask, "How can you do it?" as they observe a quiet
radiance and a sanity-balancing trust in God. And they know they
probably would be acting differently in similar situations. It's then we
have an opportunity to tell about our Father, about the always available support and reinforcement and help in time of need.

That's what a father's for. So we can quit asking, "But why, God?"

13

Who Says God Hears Me?

The scene, a public meeting. The occasion, the announced appearance of an influential personage. Drawn by the hope and expectation that he can aid them, each one comes with his own requests or grievances. Some are given a hearing, others are not.

The meeting breaks up and the crowd goes its way. A few people are satisfied, some disillusioned, and not a few bitter. As is generally true, not many took into consideration the problems connected with trying to pay attention to a large number of individual requests. Most of us are too intent on our own case, and we are all too prone to attribute negative motives to the person who has failed to hear and heed us.

"I wouldn't take that man's help now if he offered it," I've heard some disgruntled people say. It's not for us to judge their reactions or behavior. But it's sad, when, perhaps because of one or a series of such disappointing experiences, the person begins to suspect everybody—and even God, Himself—of being indifferent to his cry of need.

In effect, such a person is saying, "Why should I bother to pray to God? Who says He'll hear me?" Their problem is not that they are unable to accept things from God. It is, rather, that they have not because they ask not, as James puts it (*see* 4:2). In attributing to God the weaknesses and failings of men, they rob themselves.

There's another group who "can't take things from God." These are the cynics and skeptics. Their problem? They cannot intellectually accept the fact that God *can* hear every person's prayer. Who is to say what caused them to feel this way? It could be that everything they have ever heard or read or been taught by other people has refuted the idea of a God who bends over the parapets of heaven to hear a human cry; that no personal experiences have caused them to question the truth of such thinking.

Both types—the man who thinks God *won't* and the one who feels God *can't* hear him—can find all the assurance they need that God will hear them, that He does listen, that His ear is ever open to their cry (*see* Psalms 34:15).

To be sure, it does take faith to really believe that God is a prayer-hearing and a prayer-answering God, on a universal scale, in our era of burgeoning population, to intellectually accept Isaiah's statement,

> . . . the Lord's hand is not shortened, that it cannot save; neither his ear heavy, that it cannot hear.
>
> Isaiah 59:1

It takes faith to simply believe what the Bible is beautifully specific about, that is, until we lift the whole scene out of our own limited orbit.

We may need to take out our thoughts and dust them off and ask ourselves, "Am I transferring the problems that hinder my communication with other people, to my relationship with God?" Then do a little evaluating.

Let's look at a number of possible hindrances.

Prescribed time is one.

But God does not have "hours": no OPEN or CLOSED sign. There isn't a word in the Bible that would indicate any such thing. No appointment is needed, either day or night. God doesn't sleep, the psalmist tells us (121:4).

Another great barrier to communication is language.

God has no language problem with any of us. And think of what that embraces! All the languages and dialects of Africa (just a day or so ago, a missionary to Africa told me they have fourteen major dialects plus French, the official language, in their small country— half the size of the state of Iowa); all of India and the subcontinent's languages; Indonesia, the Latin American countries, Europe: every language under the sun, including our minority language, English. God understands us all.

Nobody on the face of the earth is excluded from approaching God due to his mother tongue. Perhaps David had this in mind when in Psalms 19 he made it abundantly clear that God communicates, through nature, to everyone under the sun:

There is no speech nor language, where their voice is not heard.

V.3

It may be mind-boggling, but it is a fact that God can and does hear us when we call.

The technically minded may toy with whether God has some kind of divine "mixer" stationed between here and heaven, a device for unifying language as it was before the Tower of Babel fiasco. Prayer would then reach God all in the same language. Fascinating speculation (which, I feel sure, does not displease God since He gave man the power to reason).

If the day ever comes—and it may indeed come before long—when man's inventiveness will have reached its zenith, when science and technology will have teamed to perfect a "man-made man," this is the factor that will still be missing: *the power to reason.* The masterpiece of computerized skill will not be made in the image of God. A holy God will not have breathed into "him" the breath of life. He will not have a free will (though the robot will *appear* to be making decisions, no doubt). And he will be lacking any semblance of ability to reason.

We have to believe that our God is smarter than the United Nations functionaries, and the UN provides a force of 75 simultaneous translators. I can trust God to have 75 billion if they were needed.

Less inquiring minds settle for "The Bible tells me so." Then, for most of us, there is the daily object lesson of the telephone, telegram, even the radio and television. Though we cannot comprehend their workings, we can appropriate their benefits. If we needed some approximation to bolster our faith, these would perhaps help us understand how God can hear us.

It's good to keep in mind that not only is God the originator of all the components of man's technology, *He is the originator of man's creativity in utilizing and developing* these components. We can be sure that He has a good system for hearing prayer, no matter how many people are on the line.

For many in our world, *place* and *position* are important to acceptable praying.

But God has not so decreed. Some feel that sitting, or standing, or kneeling is a consideration. Prone on the face five times a day is the only way to God for millions in the Muslim world (with particular attention to facing Mecca).

It would be an interesting study to find out the various places of prayer recorded in the Scriptures. A few are: the belly of a whale, (Jonah); on a river bank (Lydia); on a rooftop (Peter); in prison (Paul and Silas). Where I live, much praying is done on the freeways, not only because there is, obviously, plenty of reason to pray there, but also because the driving affords uninterrupted time for communing with God (much less distracting, I find, than listening to the news on my car radio).

The sum of biblical light on the subject would indicate that God is not so much interested in where we happen to be, or the position we assume in praying, as He is in our being aware that we *can* approach Him in prayer—always—with the assurance that He does hear us.

The matter of the *distance* between heaven and earth seems to pose a problem for some who doubt the worth of taking time to pray. For a very brief period this troubled me in the early days of my Christian life. Totally nontechnical and having an uncomplicated type of mind, I was, nevertheless, a little rocked when a person I respected gave me a little lecture on the subject. "Don't you realize," he asked, "that if Jesus had traveled at (some astronomical speed which I've forgotten because it likely didn't register on my mind) He still would not be out of the earth's atmosphere? How can you believe that Jesus is in heaven? It's a mathematical impossibility . . ." and more of the same.

This was before *Sputnik* and *Cape Canavaral* and *astronaut* invaded the language. I'm glad that the Holy Spirit didn't let me get all caught up with such reasoning. I'm satisfied that, if in our day, some of my neighbors in Pasadena can talk to people on the moon, the God who gave men the brains to conceive of and develop space technology surely can hear us. I'm not worried about God's hearing range. (As a sidelight, these Jet Propulsion Lab men are quite ordinary citizens. I happened to be with some guests at a restaurant one evening last November. Diagonally across from us at a large table some kind of celebration was going on. After a candle-lit cake had been brought to that table a cheer arose from the men. Our waitress, arriving at that moment, explained, "That's the JPL crew. They've just sent Mariner 10 up, and they're celebrating.")

As is well documented, a number of the astronauts themselves are committed Christians. Even though Russian Spaceman Titov is reputed to have said that he saw neither God nor angels in his seventeen orbits around the earth, therefore God does not exist, Christians in every generation have believed, have not stumbled over how far away heaven is, and whether God can hear us.

Time zones likewise make no difference in our access to God.

But what if they did! Pondering this one day, these lines came to me:

> What if—
> God worked in one time zone alone
> And slept the hours between?
> How could we safely rest
> East—or West?
> But God He slumbers not.

Because almost always someone dear to me is in some faraway country, I have to try to figure what time it is as I pray for them. But I never, *never* have to ponder whether or not it is God's time for hearing me where I am, and answering where my dear ones are.

Still another hindrance, in the opinion of a number of people, is that

God does not really hear them, that God doesn't read them when they pray. This just has to be unreasonable. For surely the God who made us understands us totally, as no one on earth ever can.

Even when we cannot articulate all that is in our hearts, God still hears (*see* Romans 8:26,27).

God made us for communion with Himself. None of these factors we have mentioned: prescribed time, language, location, position in prayer, the distance to heaven, time zones, or the ability to articulate —or all of these put together—can hinder us when we want to reach God in prayer.

None of these I have mentioned has been much of a personal problem to me in my Christian life. If any had been, perhaps the most persistent might have been the "Who am I that God will hear me in a crowd?"

Any such conscious or subconscious feeling would certainly have been dispelled by a spectacle I witnessed one summer day years ago.

It was blistering hot in New York City. An estimated one million people had escaped to the beaches. Each little party had established its own beachhead under the bright-hued umbrellas that suddenly mushroom on these public beaches. Radios blared. Ice-cream vendors shouted their wares. Frantic mamas, momentarily missing their small children, screamed their names. It was bedlam.

Everyone appeared oblivious of everyone else but their immediate group.

The water was thickly peopled.

Suddenly, from his tower near where we were established, a lifeguard leapt and with about six strides reached the water's edge and jumped into a skiff. Within minutes he had brought to shore a swimmer who had been in trouble; a near fatality had been averted.

On the beach that day *I* had heard no cry for help, nor had those around me. But the lifeguard had. His ear had been tuned to a cry of distress.

This is the kind of *God* we have.

Who says God hears me? God does.

Because he hath inclined his ear unto me, therefore will I call upon him as long as I live.

Psalms 116:2

The Bible offers an interesting little piece of satire that is in direct contradiction to all we know of the one true God.

It was the great showdown on Mount Carmel: Baal versus Jehovah God. When all the impassioned pleas of the prophets of Baal produced no response, Elijah suggested,

Cry aloud: for he is a god; either he is talking [someone else on the line and you can't get through] . . . or he is in a journey, or peradventure he sleepeth, and must be awaked.

1 Kings 18:27

Not so the God in whom we trust. He needs no answering service, for "His ear is ever open to our cry" (see Psalms 34:15).

14

What's a Father For?

"Look!" Joe said, not bothering to hide his hostility, "somebody sent us this." It was near Christmas and he had answered a ring of the doorbell and returned to the living room with a gift basket in his arms.

To his wife's delighted exclamations, he grunted, "Why did they have to do this? Wonder what they want from me?"

Joe is typical of the people who seem to feel there has to be an angle to any gift or favor they receive from someone. Joe never wants to take anything, no matter what the occasion.

What is this man (and others like him) really saying by this attitude, by his seeming inability to take things in a normal manner? Is he betraying his own sense of inferiority, a who-am-I-that-anybody-would-want-to-give-me-something or do-a-favor-for-me attitude? His own low self-concept tends to make him suspicious of everyone else's motives.

Another person who can't bear to take things from other people is the overly independent individual. He may have come by this independence the hard way, grubbing for everything he can call his own, and he fiercely guards against losing this independence. Or, the person might be reacting against having been overly dependent in his earlier life. I know a woman like that. For much of her life, as a minister's wife, people were always doing things for her and her family. The day came when this was no longer the case; she was on her own and she determined to prove that she could pay her own way. But she tended to overdo it, sometimes to the embarrassment of other people (someone who offered to pay a restaurant check, for example). One day after such an incident when this woman had been particularly insistent, her daughter said, "Mother, now that we're alone, do you mind if I say something?" And—a little hesitantly but sweetly—she offered her suggestion: "Mother, I think you need to learn to *take* things graciously."

The mother thought over what her daughter had said and began to appreciate it and practice the kindly offered advice. She even gained the insight to realize that not only had she been ungracious but she had been robbing her friends of the joy of giving.

If our friends feel it when we will not take things from them, how must God, our heavenly Father, feel? With a heaven full of good things to offer!

For the sad thing about these people who can't take things from other people is that they extend this same thinking into their spiritual concepts. The ultimate damage to themselves is that they cannot accept a "free salvation" (a fallacy in terms, since nothing in heaven or earth has ever cost so much as our salvation!). But these people feel that even God must have an angle, or that He is robbing them of their independence. They can only partake of what God has to offer *if they can work for it,* not internalizing Ephesians 2:8,9:

For by grace are ye saved . . . and that not of yourselves: it is the gift of God: Not of works, lest any man should boast.

God knows how prone we are to boast.
Verse 10 goes on,

For we are his workmanship, created in Christ Jesus unto good works. . . .

There's nothing wrong with good works. Good works have characterized Christian commitment throughout the centuries: schools, hospitals, orphanages, and other expressions of Christ's compassion and concern for humanity, carried on in His name.

But our good works are the outworking, not the *price* of our salvation.

Salvation by grace alone—this is the great leveler. The rich can't buy it. There's no special dispensation for the poor. And the hard-working middle class can never work hard enough or long enough to merit God's free gift of salvation. It *is* a gift. And, like every other gift, it must be received in order to be effective.

We get it from our Father.

It would appear that even God has a need, a need for us to let Him be our loving, saving, heavenly Father.

Some people will not take this gift from Him.

Along this line, a most poignant true story comes to my mind.

A father of my acquaintance wanted to give his ten-year-old son an especially memorable day. He said to the boy, "Son, I'm going to take you to the city [New York City]; we'll do all the things you want to do; go to a ball game, buy whatever you see that you would like, and we'll eat at whatever restaurant you'd like to go to. We'll have a great time!"

They started out happily, eager for a day by themselves. But every time the father suggested buying something for his son, the boy would say, "No thanks, Dad. I don't need it." Almost incredibly, the whole day went this way. The boy and his dad enjoyed the game, but even the hot dogs and soft drinks didn't interest the son more than just one time during the afternoon. Later, strolling in Times Square, the father kept seeing something he thought the boy would surely like to have. But no, he wasn't interested in getting things.

When they arrived home, the boy gave an eager account of the things they'd done and seen in the city. But his dad's rather pathos-filled comment was, "I wanted to do more and to buy him some things, but *he wouldn't take anything.*"

How much, I wonder, do we miss out on every day of our life, because we try to live independent of God's loving provision for us? The psalmist David knew all about taking things from the Lord:

> Blessed be the Lord, who daily loadeth us with benefits, even the God of our salvation.

> Psalms 68:19

David wouldn't have known about the load of benefits if he had never reached out and accepted God's offered goodness.

Another aspect is that the person who cannot take things can rarely bring himself to give to others, or even to the Lord's work, whether giving of himself or of his material goods. Such persons seem to feel, in addition to "Why would somebody want to give *me* anything?" "Why should *I* give to other people?"

So we can rob people by not being willing to let them give to us. We can likewise cheat people by our own unwillingness to give to them. So it's fortunate that a ten-year-old can be gently guided and helped so that he will grow to adulthood with healthy, balanced attitudes toward taking things from other people.

One of the most disastrous results of one's not being able or willing to take things from God occurs when we will not take His forgiveness. There are some—perhaps not too many, but even one is too many—who have lived in dreadful alienation and unhappiness because they could not forgive themselves for a particular sin. There's no way we can do this until we have first taken forgiveness from the Lord, and let Him apply the balm of Gilead to the open, festering sore of unforgiven sin.

For, again—we cannot extend genuine forgiveness to another if we cannot receive and appropriate forgiveness from God. One of the most gifted yet dwarfed and unhappy Christians I've ever known is a person who avowedly *will not* forgive a neighbor who, she feels, has wronged her. Because of this, a bitterness and sourness of spirit has taken over in her own life. Her personal happiness is nil and her witness for Christ severely limited. Concerned over this person, I find myself wondering if her deepest problem is that she has never *heard* what Jesus emphasized so plainly: "Love your neighbor *as yourself.*" Not loving herself enough to feel worthy of God's total forgiveness *and to take it from Him,* she has neither love nor forgiveness to share with a neighbor.

I also ponder at times that it may well be we will have to give account to God of how we rated in *taking,* as well as in *giving.*

Can you sense the yearning, the pathos in Christ's words, "I would have . . . and *you would not*" (*see* Matthew 23:37).

Jesus makes it amply clear how much He longed to do for those to whom He was speaking, in spite of all the black marks against them. But they:

Would not accept identification with Him.
Would not take His protection (under His wings).
Would not take daily provision.
Would not take love and caring.

What must Jesus have felt? How did God the Father feel as His Gift was spurned?

Sometimes it calls for more character to be a taker, to admit need and dependence. But—isn't that what a Father is for? In my mind I can see a little guy with a new baseball mitt or a ball. As his admiring friends gather round, he says to them (maybe with studied casualness), "My Dad gave it to me," and in the boy's face is a world of pride in his father. He knows what a father is for!

Another thing a father is for is a little harder to take. A father is for authority. I recently received an article on this subject from Dr. Norvell Peterson, a psychiatrist in Massachussetts. He wrote of a father as God's surrogate; the father as a stand-in for God and particularly in the matter of authority.

I have always been impressed with the emphasis God places on the father's role in the home. Remember when He said of Abraham,

> I know him, that he will command his children and his household after him, and they shall keep the way of the Lord, to do justice and judgment. . . .
>
> Genesis 18:19

Abraham was destined by God for immortality—". . . all the nations of the earth shall be blessed in him" (v.18). But to God, it was all-important that Abraham be a good *father* and a responsible head of the house, using his God-given authority. That's what a father is for.

The New Testament has the same requirements for the man who would aspire to being a Christian leader.

> One that ruleth well his own house, having his children in subjection with all gravity; (For if a man know not how to rule his own house, how shall he take care of the church of God?).
>
> I Timothy 3:4,5

Obviously the intent is that the Christian leader will not be denying before his children the things he preaches and emphasizes in the church. We can only speculate as to how many young people from Christian homes have been turned off because of what they see as a double standard.

Some fathers do a terrific job of representing God to their children. Others fail miserably—and this doesn't make God look good.

Increasingly, Christian psychologists and psychiatrists and pastors are finding that a great problem area in a young person's relationship with God is that he never had a good relationship with his own father, God's stand-in. As a result, these young people find it hard to take anything from God—even His *love*.

Whatever the reasons that keep us from being able to take things from the Lord, resulting in other negatives in our lives, happily we can change. The adage, "While there's life there's hope," can also apply to the possibility of new, changed attitudes.

It pays to take out our feelings, ideas, prejudices, and reasoning and evaluate them, mentally finger and handle them, acquaint ourselves with them. Plato, in his defense of Socrates, spoke well when he said, "The life which is unexamined is not worth living."

When we do "examine ourselves" (as Saint Paul likewise recommended in another frame of reference—*see* I Corinthians 11:28), we can then ask God to give us clear vision of what we are, in the light of what He would have us to be. And we can begin to deliberately work at shedding the things that do not make us happy about ourselves as we are.

Emphasis must be on the *self*-examination; not, "I see where Tom needs to get rid of certain things in his life," or "Mary would certainly be a better person if she would change." This kind of thinking offers us no help for change ourselves.

I know a Christian woman who has a nice balance. She says, "I don't take a basket to church with me to bring home everything the minister says. It's not *all* for me. But neither do I carry a shovel to toss it all to the people on either side of me, for some of the sermon *is* for me; I need to take it to heart."

One day as she examined herself in the light of what she had heard in God's house, she saw something she did not like. She recognized that she had been somewhat unkind to one of her young pupils in Sunday school that morning. So right after dinner she hied herself to the child's home and (a very difficult thing for this rather proud and conservative woman) she admitted to the parents, and asked the little girl's forgiveness for her ungracious attitude that day. In this she was rooting out something that self-examination had shown her was there. In its place she had planted some fruit of the Spirit. She had recognized the need for change and had done something about it.

Some people never come to this place of increasing maturity. They justify themselves and their behavior and attitudes with, "That's how the Lord made me and that's the way I am."

Not always do people blame the Lord. Some attribute all their bad points to their parents, or their background. (A TV and radio commentator, the late Joe Pyne, used to say that psychiatry is "lying on a couch squealing on your mother.")

Rather than attributing our negative qualities to one source or another, we might do better to ask ourselves these few questions:

Do I like myself as I am?
Can I admire the *me* I know myself to be?
Am I content to settle for this *me* for the rest of my life?
If I would like to change, how honest am I about intending to try?

Fortunately, personality is not static. Also, we can be sure that God is interested in our changing. He is willing and eager and has provided the elements needed for change. The big thing we need is to be humble enough to take these good things from Him. What's a Father for?

And God our Father has no angles, no ulterior motives. He is only interested in blessing us by helping us to become a little more like Jesus.

15

Acceptance Spells Peace

We frequently deplore the volume of advertising that bombards us but we can sometimes learn from it.

To illustrate: The man in the ad recoils from the shock and blinks a time or two. Then, recovering somewhat, he says to the person who has just administered the unexpected treatment, "Thanks. I needed that."

Think of the implications of such a statement when carried over into the realm of Christian living!

Inherent in the person's response is an admission that although the momentary shock of the experience was not pleasant, the aftereffect was good; the uncomfortable seconds were a prelude to better feelings.

Where have we heard that before (and not from Madison Avenue)?

Long before the era of our modern media, Paul the Apostle wrote out of deep experience,

> . . . our light affliction, which is but for a moment, worketh for us a far more exceeding and eternal weight of glory.
>
> 2 Corinthians 4:17

In essence, Paul is saying, "It's not pleasant, but—thanks, God. I needed it."

Does this, perhaps, strike you as something of a Pollyanna attitude? Are you thinking, Next thing you know they'll be quoting "All things work together for good"?

How can trouble or trial turn out for the best?

This is a normal, human question. And some people really get hung up on it. They wonder if other people are being strictly honest when they say, "Thank You, God, for sending me this trial." To them this seems a bit phony, or at best a hyperpious attitude.

Because it is a fact of life that no one completely escapes some trials and problems, it's certainly worth thinking over how a Christian should act—and react—in the midst of them.

What are the options?

A trial comes, some problem confronts us—and two courses are open to each one of us.

We can resist. Or we can accept what comes our way.

A form of resistance, though not always recognized as such, is allowing ourselves to sink into a Slough of Despond. There, Self-Pity, first cousin to Despondency, soon sucks us still further down, until we are wallowing in it. Our song is "Poor me. No one ever had to bear such a trial as I'm going through; God must have forgotten me, or forsaken me."

By reacting to trouble in this fashion, we are virtually criticizing God, verbally doubting His love and downgrading His ability to care for us even if He does still love us. In a sense we are tossing God's promises in His face.

All this does is compound the problem. For now, in addition to having to handle it on our own, we are deliberately fracturing our relationship with the Lord. Surely doubt and disbelief grieve the Holy Spirit of God. In fact, *we can only grieve one who loves us,* so how much power is ours to grieve the very heart of God with our doubting His love?

The alternative course?

Acceptance. We can take the circumstance and in faith say, "Thanks, God. I know it will work out for good." Oh, at the time it takes all the faith we can muster to enable us to see the silver lining in the cloud-dimmed skies. It's true that we don't know at times why God sends trials our way. But faith's alternative to *Why* is *Thank You, God*—even when, smarting under the blow of circumstances, we may feel more like defiantly striking back than saying *Thank You, God.*

Built into our attitude of acceptance is our acknowledgement that God is working out His will in our lives; that:

> He knows; He loves; He cares;
> Nothing this truth can dim.
> God gives the very best to those
> Who leave the choice to Him.

So, in accepting what God sends our way we are telling Him, "I know You are Sovereign. You created me. Through faith in Your Son I became a member of Your family—and *You are love*. Even though I do not understand this particular thing You're doing in my life, I know You, Lord. I know You have my interests at heart and that You are doing this for my ultimate good."

Moreover, has it ever occurred to you that God does not have to explain His actions to us any more than the potter has to explain to the clay he is molding. God does not have to answer our often petulant *why*. Many times He does sooner or later reveal the *why*, but faith and trust do not sit back, withholding acceptance until we have the explanation.

How does acceptance pay off?

With the commitment of our way to God comes a draining of any resentment or rebellion against our circumstances. And this magic of acceptance is more than a spiritual concept or theory. As many in the field of psychiatry and psychology have long known and some are just beginning to recognize, *acceptance engenders peace.*

Amy Carmichael, in one of her unforgettable poems, expresses this so eloquently. Having worked in sequence through the areas of forgetting, endeavor, aloofness, and submission in a person's quest for peace, she concludes each stanza with "Vain the word . . ." until she comes to the final lines:

> I will *accept* the breaking sorrow
> Which God, tomorrow
> Will to His son explain.
> *Then* did the turmoil deep

> Within him cease.
> Not vain the word, *not* vain—
> For *in acceptance lieth peace.*

The famed missionary wrote well and truly. Acceptance does beget peace; acceptance has both emotional and physical ramifications, in addition to the better recognized spiritual benefits. For it takes emotional energy to fight an inward battle as when we figuratively bang our heads against the brick wall of circumstances in which we find ourselves. The same measure of acceptance applied to the situation would leave us in a much better state to be able to deal with it.

Why does acceptance bring such positive results?

We may not know or understand all the dynamics at work. But when we know God and trust Him, we realize that He knows what is best for us.

It's no idle whim that causes God to bid us give thanks *in everything.* (The little word *in* is worth noting in this context.) God doesn't tell us to give thanks for everything—that might be too hard for most of us. In everything give thanks, He says: while we are in the midst of the experience.

Giving thanks and acceptance cannot be separated from each other. Saying, "Thanks, God. I needed that," has in it seeds of gratitude as well as faith and hope: faith that God is working out His plan in our life; hope for the good outcome because our Father can be trusted to do what is best for us.

This is where Romans 8:28 with it's "all things work together for good" comes in. The individual components of a situation in which we find ourselves may not be good, but as God works them together they produce His good design. Any homemaker can readily understand this concept. Take, for instance, the separate ingredients of a cake and try feeding them to you family. Baking powder or soda, raw eggs, flour, shortening: ugh! I can hear the comments. But we don't dish up those components. We mix them and let them "work together" for the prescribed time, then we delight our family with the result.

In like manner, while it is true that *things* don't work for us, *God works* in the midst of the *things* for our good.

When we can see this, we can be thankful for what God is doing with us, and in us and through us. It's when we accept what He sends, when we cast all the responsibility for what happens to us upon God, that we are conserving rather than draining our own resources. More than that, we find that in thus casting our burden on the Lord, we actually recharge our spiritual and emotional batteries. And the results to the physical are also on the plus side.

What can be more valuable than a calm attitude in a time of trouble or crisis? The Christian, operating from a platform of inner peace, should mirror this calm more than anyone else. Why then do not more of us latch onto this great potential? Paul speaks strongly to this point:

> Don't worry about anything; instead, pray about everything; tell God your needs and don't forget to thank him for his answers. If you do this you will experience God's peace, which is far more wonderful than the human mind can understand.

> Philippians 4:6,7 LB

I admit that it's a great mystery how this can be. But I know from experience that it is true. In fact one of the greatest discoveries I have ever made is that a Christian *can* know real peace—genuine soul- and mind-calming peace—even while he still has the problem that should (humanly speaking) shatter his peace. The open secret? Acceptance.

The question arises: Must we expect trials as Christians? Does God delight in showering trouble on us?

No, of course He does not. Nevertheless, the Scriptures are honest and realistic in preparing us to expect trouble: "In the world ye shall have tribulation," we read in John 16:33, and the Speaker is our Lord Himself. (The inference appears to be that the tribulation is tied into the fact that we are in the world, that human beings by virtue of just being alive can expect some trials.) This applies both to the Christian and to the non-Christian, as evidenced by Job's statement (5:7),

... man is born unto trouble, as the sparks fly upward.

Our first parents defied God and thereby defiled their perfect environment. Ever since, as the Bible makes clear, "the whole creation groans" (*see* Romans 8:22). So it's no wonder that people, likewise, groan.

As one of my much loved pastors, a man who helped me immensely at the start of my Christian life, frequently quoted,

> The whole creation groans
> And waits to hear the Voice
> That shall restore her comeliness
> And make its wastes rejoice.
> Come, Lord, and sweep away
> The sin, the scars, the stain,
> And make this blighted world of ours
> Thine own fair world again.
>
> JAMES MCFARLANE

That day will come—but it is not yet! So people universally suffer.

It's true that people can and do create their own suffering, many times. One way we do this is through abuse of the body which God has given us, this "temple of the Holy Spirit." We can do this daily through excesses of one kind or another. We need to be honest and face up to this possibility before looking around for someone or something to blame when we suffer some trial. In particular, we should be slow to conclude that God sent the trial, thus excusing ourselves.

In special ways, however, the Christian can expect to face difficulties along the way to the celestial city. We journey through hostile territory, for Satan is the prince of this world and he only yields after fierce contest. He works day and night, 365 days a year, making this world an uncomfortable place for those who love the Lord Jesus and are interested in living for Him.

The fact of suffering as par for the Christian's course came as no surprise to the Apostle Paul. It was defined for him as a part of his special assignment and commission from Christ:

... he [Paul] is a chosen vessel unto me, to bear my name before the Gentiles. . . . I will shew him how great things he must suffer for my name's sake.

Acts 9:15,16

We do an injustice to new converts when we create (knowingly or unknowingly) the impression that "Now that you're a Christian you will never have any more problems."

Far from resisting such a concept, from resenting that he was expected to suffer in this life on which he had embarked, Paul accepted suffering as an honor, as a badge of identification with Jesus Christ. Paul shared this belief with his beloved Philippian brethren:

... to you has been given the privilege not only of trusting him but also of suffering for him.

Philippians 1:29 LB

Suffering—a privilege!

Some people suffer more than others, as believers. And sometimes we hear of "the school of suffering": this would say to us that God is educating those whom He calls to bear particular trials. Enrolled in this school, we can be sure we have the Master Teacher.

God is also the Master Designer. He knows best how to perfect that which He has created. God is not toying with ceramics. He is molding us for eternity. And this is not always a pleasant experience for us at the time. We don't always feel like saying, "Thanks, God. I needed that."

But—and we will never be able in a thousand eternities to understand or explain this—there's a wonderful, divine alchemy that produces sweetness out of sorrow, peace out of pain, and beauty from ashes. Who will dispute that this is so? The serenity on the face of the chronic sufferer, the peace-filled expression when pain furrows, would be more understandable to the bystander: these eloquently voice another truth Paul came to see. It's this:

My grace is sufficient for thee.

2 Corinthians 12:9

Surely this is the peace that passes understanding. And it emanates from acceptance of the situation as part of God's total, loving plan.

Unquestionably the most difficult thing to accept—*to thank God for* —is death. We know intellectually that it is appointed unto man once to die. We know spiritually that to die is gain, that absence from the body means being present with the Lord. As Christians we would strongly defend our position on this truth. But we have our emotions to deal with. Our emotions tell us that the last enemy is death, and we shrink from this enemy.

The medical profession has long known that normally there are three reactions on the part of someone who realizes (or is told) that his death is imminent. The first is *unbelief:* "Everybody dies. I know that. But not me—not now!" The second reaction is that the patient looks around for someone to *blame.* The physician comes in for more than his share of this blame: "There must be something you've done or failed to do for me, doctor." Thirdly, is *acceptance.* After a while, when the idea of dying has become somewhat less of a shock, some people are able to draw from an inner reserve the ability to accept the fact that their remaining days on earth will be few. And with this acceptance—this cease-fire against the inevitable—comes a measure of peace.

Clearly, then, it should follow that when the patient is a true believer in Christ, as he accepts his impending departure from this life, his peace will be *the peace that Jesus gives.* He will be enveloped, blanketed in it, knowing that "neither life nor death can separate him from the love of God that is in Christ Jesus" (*see* Romans 8:38,39). To a degree he may muster the dying grace and faith to say, "I thank You, God."

Not all trials, however, come in the form of physical suffering. Some are emotional, some may even be spiritual, and for some people trials are a combination of all three. Some problems call for the help of

professional counselors: not only the medical doctor but the psychiatrist or psychologist and the pastor. But, ultimately, whatever the
problem, if there is to be healing there must first be acceptance. And
when this acceptance is based on "in everything give thanks," how
great are the resources for healing.

Then, because God is the Author of order and purpose, the one who
has been enabled to triumph over suffering begins to see what God had
in mind in permitting the trial. A new spiritual awareness is emerging
and with it a new compassion for others.

How do I know these things? A young pastor asked me that question one day. I didn't have to ponder long before replying. How did
I learn the enduring worth of having a spirit of thankfulness, of being
able to accept what God sends into my life? It hasn't been so much
a matter of learning but of *proving* it. How do we prove things?
Generally by testing them.

Many a Christian can live a lifetime without coming to understand
how powerful is the Word of God, how unfailing God's promises. I
was almost one of them.

I recall when one of the finest men in our church died very suddenly. The family and ours were more than fellow Christians; our
relationship closer than that between most pastors and church members. For a number of weeks the new widow daily came to our home.
She and I would sit by the hour and talk as we drained the tea-
pot.

Some years passed and again our paths crossed. She was eager to
tell me of her life in those intervening years. In the course of the
conversation I said, "Ruth, I sometimes think of those times you came
to my home so desperately in need of help. How much like sounding
brass and tinkling symbol my words must have been to you. How
could I know how you were hurting? I had never known a severe trial
in my whole life (and I had added, 'God was good to me')."

My friend was gracious. She smiled and said, "I knew you didn't
understand—but you *loved* me, and *gave me your time.*"

"Yes," I answered, "and you probably went somewhere else for
your *comfort.*"

I really had thought that God was good to me in not letting life buffet me. I know better now. For, in His love and wisdom God did send (or permit: I'm no theologian) crushing sorrow that threatened to knock the spiritual props from under me. Rebellion, resentment against God, self-pity, depression—I've been through them all. Meanwhile the covenant-keeping God did not forsake me. It took time for me to see anything at all to be thankful for. As for acceptance, who could accept such a trial? It was too much for God to expect that I would. But the Lord is patient. He knows our frame and He is of great compassion.

It was a gradual process, but the day came when I could actually say, "Thank You, God. I needed that." With the acceptance came *new joy,* a new understanding of the love of God, a new relationship with Him, and a new ability to understand other people and to be compassionate toward them. The Living Bible beautifully expresses this in 2 Corinthians 1:3,4:

What a wonderful God we have—he is the Father of our Lord Jesus Christ, the source of every mercy, and the one who so wonderfully comforts and strengthens us in our hardships and trials. And why does he do this? So that when others are troubled, needing our sympathy and encouragement, we can pass on to them this same help and comfort God has given us.

The truth of these words is personalized for us; we see God's sweet uses of adversity when *in acceptance* we have found His *peace.*

My own concept of acceptance and trust and taking things as from the Lord is strengthened, my faith reassured by the words of Dr. Ralph Keiper, of the Conservative Baptist Seminary in Denver, Colorado, and well-known Bible teacher:

Trusting the Lord is not theoretical. Trusting the Lord is accepting yourself for what you are. And the way you can do this is to realize that the One who counts most has accepted you, even God the Father. And the guarantee is Calvary, and the Holy Spirit wants you to know you are accepted in the beloved.

It's not hard to take this kind of acceptance—God being willing to accept us—and as we take this from the Lord, our acceptance spells peace.